EMPTY NEST, FULL LIFE

Empty Nest Full Life

Anne Marie Drew

DIMENSIONS
FOR LIVING

NASHVILLE

EMPTY NEST, FULL LIFE

Copyright © 1995 by Dimensions for Living

This book is printed on acid-free, recycled paper.

Library of Congress Cataloging-in-Publication Data

Drew, Anne Marie.
    Empty Nest, Full Life / Anne Marie Drew.
       p. cm.
    ISBN 0-687-00100-5 (alk. paper)
      1. Empty nesters—Religious life. 2. Middle aged women—
Religious life. 3. Mothers—Religious life. I. Title.
    BV4527.4.D74   1995
    248.8'431—dc20   94-33044
                                                    CIP

Unless otherwise noted, Scripture quotations are from the *Holy Bible:
New International Version*. Copyright © 1973, 1978, 1984 by the International Bible Society. Used by permission of Zondervan Bible Pub-
lishers.

Those noted NRSV are from the New Revised Standard Version Bible,
copyright © 1989, by the Division of Christian Education of the
National Council of the Churches of Christ in the United States of
America. Used by permission.

The story on page 12 is from Anthony de Mello's book *Sadhana: A
Way to God.*

95 96 97 98 99 00 01 02 03 04—10 9 8 7 6 5 4 3 2 1

MANUFACTURED IN THE UNITED STATES OF AMERICA

To

ANTHONY AND JOSEPH

"now grown in grace / Equal with wondering"

CONTENTS

ACKNOWLEDGMENTS

To the following people "I can no other answer make but thanks/ And thanks, and ever thanks":

The many women who talked to me as I worked on this book. By talking about themselves and their families with such candor and openness, they helped me to understand the empty nest in new ways.

My sister, Charlotte, my lifelong companion and my best editor.

The wide array of students who've traveled through my life in the past few years. Their stories, their casual comments, their good humor are woven into these pages. I am especially grateful to the U.S. Naval Academy Masqueraders, Class of 1994—a sterling group of students, who often made me forget the word *empty*.

My own parents who remind me of the perseverance of God's love.

My daughter, Francesca, who knows about the Sea of Galilee.

INTRODUCTION

Two words have been bothering me lately. I do not like the sound of them. I don't know who invented this phrase, but I wish I'd never heard it: *empty nest*. Even the sight of the words in print bothers me.

My children are leaving home. I have a supportive husband, a dream job, good health, an abiding faith—but my children are packing up their belongings and moving away. And the simple question—"Mom, can you pick up some more empty boxes when you go grocery shopping?"—reduces me to tears.

"No," I want to tell my children, "I don't want to collect empty boxes so that you can pack your CD's and posters and sweatshirts into them. No, I will not help you pull the Cleveland Browns pennants from your bedroom walls. And I will not help load the car."

But, of course, I even supply the packing tape—the final reminder that my years of raising children are nearly finished.

Soon, I will have an empty nest.

Wasn't it just yesterday that I longed for an hour to myself? Wasn't I the one who thought, "If only I could get dressed up without having a baby drool all over my blouse"? How many times, through the years, did I pray for peace, quiet, and more control over my own schedule? Well, now that my prayers are about to be answered, I can't figure out why I'm not happier.

Sometimes sadness almost overwhelms me. I feel as if I am in the bottom of a deep well, disconnected from all the love, laughter, and joy that the years of raising children brought me. But then I remember something that I once heard Corrie ten Boom say in a Billy Graham movie: "There is no well so deep that He is not deeper still."

And so, I am slowly coming to understand that the empty nest is an opportunity to find God in new ways. It gives me yet another chance—and I need so many of these chances—to transform my own feeble heart into the heart of Jesus Christ. As my sons and daughter are called to their own adult journeys, I am being called to a deeper and closer relationship with the God who created my family. Getting accustomed to an empty nest will take some adjustment, but the God who sustained me through my fears of childbirth, through endless days of diapers, and through the years of three teenagers learning to drive—this God will not abandon me now.

Anthony de Mello tells the following story, which forever changed my concept of empty:

A priest noticed an empty chair at the bedside of a home-bound patient he went to visit. The priest asked the patient what the chair was doing there. The patient said, "I had placed Jesus on that chair and was talking to him before you arrived. . . . For years I found it extremely difficult to pray until a friend explained to me that prayer was a matter of talking to Jesus. He told me to place an empty chair nearby, to imagine Jesus sitting on that chair, and to speak with him and listen to what he says to me in reply. I've had no difficulty praying ever since." Some days later, so the story goes, the daughter of the patient came to the rectory to inform the priest that her father died. She said, "I left him alone for a couple of hours. He seemed so peaceful. When I got back to the room I found him dead. I noticed a strange thing, though; his head was resting not on the bed but on a chair that was beside his bed."

The nest, like the chair, is not really empty. It is filled with ways to draw closer to the heart of Jesus Christ.

Of course, the empty nest does not empty all at once, and this book is intended for women at all stages of the process. Everyone from the woman whose first child is about to leave to the mother whose children are already gone will find this book a companion for the journey. Married moms and single moms, career women and full-time homemakers—all will hear their stories echoed in the voices of the many women who talk about their lives in this book. The prayer exercises at the end of each chapter are designed to help in the process of drawing closer to Jesus Christ and of discerning his will for our lives.

This dual process is one of the greatest adventures that God holds out for us. Like all of life's challenges, the empty nest can be met with courage and grace and dignity. In talking to women of all ages and all walks of life, I came to understand that when children leave home, we become free in new ways. My many interviews with other women taught me that we face an exciting opportunity as we begin life anew without full-time mothering responsibilities. Free to embrace God and our world in expansive ways that were not possible when our children were at home, we can accomplish great things for the kingdom of God.

The world needs the patience we learned in the wee hours of the morning as we rocked our newborn babies. Our friends need the good humor that came to our aid when a child left an ink marker in his jeans pocket. So many places in the universe need our joy—the great joy that made us delight in a Bible-school marigold planted in a styrofoam cup.

Everything we learned and everything we became in the years of child raising has prepared us for the great adventure of the empty nest. The empty nest is not an end. It is the best of beginnings.

CHAPTER 1

WHY IS *EMPTY* SUCH A FRIGHTENING WORD?

At a cast party in late November I met the mothers of several of my students. These women had come from all over the country to watch their sons and daughters perform in a play I'd directed. The moms and I gathered at a table in a restaurant while the students congregated at the other end of the room, laughing and celebrating their theatrical success.

We were just casually talking about children leaving home when one woman said, "My oldest daughter left two years ago and I still haven't gotten over it." Another woman, with tears forming in her eyes, pointed to her son across the restaurant and said, "My son doesn't want to worry me, so he never tells me anything. But I miss him so much. I even miss worrying about him."

None of us had ever met. We came from many different towns and cities, but within minutes of being introduced we were exchanging stories about what it's like to endure children leaving home.

I came to understand that my fears and my sadness are shared by many women. Each woman told her own story about the sometimes sudden and often overwhelming sadness.

"The other day I was grocery shopping," a woman from Arizona said, "and I picked up some chocolate chip cookies from the shelf because they're my oldest son's favorite. But just as I went to put them in my cart, I remembered that my son doesn't live at home anymore. I started to cry right there in the supermarket."

Another woman from Minnesota, nodding in sympathy, said, "Last week I was looking for my car in the parking lot at the mall. I thought I spotted it—a white Toyota—so I opened the rear door to put my packages inside. But there on the backseat were two infant car seats. The car wasn't mine. I haven't needed infant seats in twenty years. I suddenly felt so empty and so lost."

The conversation, oddly enough, gave me great hope. These women were vibrant, funny, and caring, yet they, like me, could be overcome by sadness.

The painful reminders often catch me off guard, too.

One evening my daughter was babysitting in our home for an adorable, redheaded three-year-old. He was a blue-eyed little fellow, very slow to warm up but, once warmed, a real bundle of life. My daughter and I were playing a vigorous game of hide-and-seek with him. He was whipping around our den, giggling and dragging his beloved blanket behind him. His giggles and squeals filled up the room. Suddenly, our front door opened. The three-year-old stopped running and yelled, "Hey, my mom's here." With that announcement he ran into the arms of his mother.

Seeing that little boy with his arms around his mother's neck, gently winding his pudgy fingers into her hair, made me ache. I remembered the warm feel of my own toddlers in my arms.

Little, domestic incidents often drive home the loss. Gloria, a mother of two sons, remembers making dinner shortly after her first son, David, left home. "I always make those little hot dog things," she said. "You know, where you wrap the crescent roll around the hot dog. Well, a package of crescent rolls makes eight of those, and my husband and I and the boys usually had two apiece. The first time I made them after David left, my husband and other son and I each took our two hot dogs, and there were two left over on the plate. Those two stupid hot dogs sitting all alone on that plate made me cry. I had to leave the dinner table."

Cynthia, a school secretary, recalls setting the dinner table after the first of her five daughters left home. "I kept setting seven places," she said. "Five girls. Two parents. Just like always. Removing that extra place setting was so hard. It made me miss her so much."

Stephanie, a buddy of mine from high school, misses her son on Saturdays when she wants to borrow his clothes. "He always had so many of those great, oversized flannel shirts. I'd often borrow one on the weekends just to goof around in."

We experience a normal sense of loss when people move away from our immediate universe. After all, in loving our children, we pour our energy and affection and care upon them. We still have all that energy and affection and care, even when they are no longer there to receive them.

WHO NEEDS ME NOW?

I have been trying very hard lately—almost as if it were an equation I had to solve—to figure out exactly what it is that I am afraid of.

It's not only that I'll miss my children's noise and confusion, although I certainly will. It's not that I want more children, although the thought of adopting has crossed my mind. Even my daughter announced the other day, "Mom, you better adopt somebody when we're all gone. You're going to go nuts without us."

No, I do not want another child.

Part of my dread of the empty nest stems from a very real dislike of a physically empty house.

During my college years I worked the night shift, 11:00 to 7:00, as a nurse's aide in a hospital. The head nurse on the outgoing shift always gave a report on patient conditions to the incoming shift. There was one particular nurse, in her late forties, on the 3:00 to 11:00 shift that everyone on the night shift disliked. When she gave the report she took far too long. Even the most caring and thorough of nurses could give the report in ten minutes. The 3:00 to 11:00 nurses were always eager to get out of the hospital to go home. This dreaded nurse, however, regularly took a full twenty minutes to talk about the patients. Those of us on the incoming shift, believing that this woman was oblivious to the irritation she caused, grew bored and became anxious to start our nightly routine.

One night, this woman, an attractive and elegant brunette, said very quietly, "There is no reason for me to hurry home. My husband is dead and my last daughter left home three months ago." Her words were deliberate and pointed. As a smug college student who'd just kissed my boyfriend good night in the hospital parking lot, I heard her words, but failed to understand them.

Now, years later, I understand. My empty house, too, could be barren and sterile and lonely. Something else, however, cuts even closer to my arteries.

For the two decades that I've been a mother, I've been the "hub of a wheel," to borrow Anne Morrow Lindbergh's phrase. Everything in my family ran because I was connected to it. What I failed to realize is how attached I'd become to that role.

How routinely I'd say to one of my colleagues, "I can't go to the party Saturday night. One of my kids has

18

a baseball game." How often I'd say to my sisters on the phone, "I can't talk. I have to get dinner on the table early because we've got to go to a school play." Those phrases became part of my existence, without my realizing the sense of importance they gave me.

Now, there are hours on end when I'm no longer the hub. My older son left three years ago. My second son left the following year. My daughter—how can this be?—will be gone next year.

Too often, now, I walk in the door and there is no one there. I try to hear the voice of God reassuring me, "Do not be afraid, for I am with you" (Isa. 43:5a), but sometimes, even God's voice cannot fill the loneliness.

These days, when I'm driving home from work, I must face the fact that no one will ask how the day has been. My oldest son won't be there to tell me a joke or complain about his physics teacher. My second son won't be practicing the trumpet or playing Mozart's "Turkish Rondo" on the piano. And my daughter won't be waiting to ask if she can borrow a pair of earrings.

One Friday I headed home early. I had hurried a talkative student out of my office, picked up a couple of pizzas, and zipped home. My husband, Dan, would rent some videos, I figured. Then whichever kids were around would sprawl all over the family room, watching the movies with Dan and me, as we snuggled under the comforter on the sofa.

But when I walked into the house, juggling the pizza boxes with my briefcase, no one was there. The house was empty.

I'd forgotten that my daughter was spending the night with her best friend. My son was at work. My husband, a minister, had a wedding rehearsal. Friday night loomed ahead.

At first, I tried to tell myself, "Oh, an evening alone.

How nice." After all, like many women, I certainly had longed for solitude in the past.

I settled under the comforter by myself, ate a piece of pizza, and clicked on Dan Rather to watch the evening news. I felt completely and complacently relaxed.

But then Dan Rather gave his signature sign-off, "And that's part of our world tonight," and the news was done. I turned off the TV, and the house seemed full of its emptiness. The very molecules seemed to hang in the air. No voices. No long bodies stretched out on the floor.

I suddenly caught a glimpse of what my life might be like in the future, and I hated it, really hated it. Because right then, no one else's existence depended on me. I did not have to cook dinner. No one needed a ride back to school for a play rehearsal. No one needed help writing a paper. No one needed me to sign a permission slip. No one even needed to borrow my car. Everyone in my family, at that particular moment, was doing fine without me.

The surprise here for me—and I can only hope that this doesn't sound silly—is that I never knew I was so attached to being a mother. Oh, I've always cherished my children and been proud of them and enjoyed their company. But, somehow, I didn't understand that my identity was so meshed with theirs.

One day at a play rehearsal I was talking to one of my colleagues about my oldest son. A startled student, over-hearing the conversation, interrupted me in mid sentence to ask, "You've got kids? Gee, I didn't know that."

I felt as if he'd slapped me.

Me? Not have kids? I thought my kids' images were imprinted on my soul, just as their photographs are sprinkled all over my office. Anyone looking at me should be able to tell that I'm a mother, I thought.

20

The loss of identity is what cuts me the deepest. As I look at myself in the mirror, and ask myself, "What is it that you're really afraid of?" the answer comes clear: I am afraid that I won't really matter to anyone anymore.

Yes, my husband and friends and parents and students and sisters will still be precious to me. But my sense of identity is most closely tied to my role as a mother. For years, my kids have been at the core of my life. They were interested in the stories I told about my students. When I left on a trip, my daughter would hide little drawings in my suitcase that I'd find when I unpacked. When I returned home, the whole crew waited for me at the airport. Never was I one of those forlorn travelers who had no one waiting to greet them. Most of my joys and sorrows were shared with my children. If I got sick, my kids cared, even if only because it meant I couldn't cook dinner. If I stopped functioning, someone's life would be upset. My existence mattered because it mattered to my children.

Certainly, I will miss my children's confusion, their vitality, their friends, their activities. I will miss having someone try to convince me, yet again, that MTV is an art form. I will miss having my son, the high-school accounting student, patiently explain to me why I should balance my checkbook instead of trusting to fate. And when she leaves me, in too short of awhile, I will miss my daughter's ability to help me put together an outfit that isn't too pathetic looking. My children are such good companions, such kindred spirits. But missing them is not the greatest fear. Being unimportant is.

Many women express a similar fear. Christine, a school secretary whose oldest son will leave home in one year, told me, "I know my husband loves me. But somehow this doesn't have anything to do with my husband. My kids are part of me. They always have been. Loving my husband isn't the same as loving my kids."

21

Empty Nest, Full Life

Judith Viorst, in her book *Necessary Losses*, expresses the pain so well:

> Although empty nests have advantages, we will need to adapt to no longer being the heads of a throbbing, blooming, sneakers-all-over-the-living room household, to no longer being—and never again to be—that unique and special mom of "I'll ask my mom."

Every fall as kids leave home and moms lose their special and unique status, newspapers run articles about the process of children moving away. One woman described her experience to *The Baltimore Sun:* "It's terrible. I had to go to bed and stay there all day. I know intellectually that there are things left for me to do. But also I just feel like there is a tremendous void. I don't feel like anybody needs me anymore."

When I was in high school, there was a television commercial that targeted such women. A middle-aged brunette announced to the camera that when her kids left home she shed a few tears, lost ten pounds, colored her hair, and got a new job. With her last line she flung a sweater over her shoulder and sauntered saucily out the front door. As a teenager, I thought the commercial was just plain dumb. I did not care about this lady who had nothing better to do with her time than cry because her kids were leaving home. And, I was too smart to believe that dyeing her hair made a difference.

Now, twenty-five years later, I want to find that woman and ask her: Did dyeing your hair really work? I'd almost be willing to dye my hair, if that would do the trick.

But my hair color doesn't need to change. I do. I have to find God in the emptying of my nest. Just the way I found God when I went through labor.

I find myself resisting the process. I don't want a deeper union with my creator. I want all three of my kids sitting at my dinner table with my husband and me. I don't want to spend my extra time praying. I want to be working the concession stand at the Little League baseball park, selling hot dogs, and making sure not to miss my son's turn at bat.

But the days of Little League and five people at the dinner table are gone.

We have to balance the external changes in our households with internal changes. Turning to God helps us to negotiate the transitions in our families.

WHO DO YOU SAY THAT I AM?

Letting go of our children is a radical opportunity to grow in the knowledge of who we are as we stand before God.

God does not view us first and foremost as mothers. Nothing temporal—no degree, no job, not even our beloved children—alters who we are before God. When we face God, we may well have to give an accounting of ourselves as mothers, but when Jesus Christ asks of us as he did of Peter, "Who do you say that I am?" we had better not reply, "I've been too busy missing my kids to figure it out."

Perhaps the empty nest is a necessary reminder that the journey to God is a solitary one. First and foremost in this life, we are called to know and love and serve God. Our children's leaving home, painful though it is, gives us the chance to draw closer to the God who always beckons. The theologian Pierre Teilhard de Chardin encourages us to believe in the slow work of God. His advice applies to us mothers as we struggle with the changes facing us. "Give our Lord the benefit of believing that His hand is leading you," de Chardin writes, "and accept the anxiety of feeling yourself in suspense and incomplete." Trusting to God's guiding hand is essential. We have to remain confident that the comforting words from Jeremiah hold true: "'For I know the plans I have for you,' declares the LORD, 'plans to prosper you and not to harm you, plans to give you hope and a future'" (29:11).

Two favorite photos help me to visualize my journey as one full of hope.

In the first photograph, I sit beaming in an overstuffed armchair. My five-month-old daughter is on my lap. My left arm is wrapped around my two-year-old son, "the blond bomber." My four-year-old son sits on the right arm of the chair, leaning against my shoulder. All three of my "munchkins" are within my reach.

That was a long time ago.

The second picture is just me, standing all alone on top of a moor in England. Above me is sky, beneath me only the earth. My children are on the other side of the Atlantic, far beyond the reach of my arms. In this picture, too, I am smiling.

The two photos, separated as they are by the better part of two decades, visually remind me of my journey to God.

Photographs help so many women remember the love of God that has enfolded and sustained them. When Sharon, a mother of two grown children, moved into a brand new home with her husband, she decided not to devote a wall to family photos. Sharon explained, "In our old house we always had a wall of family photos. I thought I was tired of them. And our new house was so pretty and clean, I didn't want to clutter up a wall with pictures of baseball teams and senior proms. But you know what happened? I missed those pictures. After two weeks in our new house, I actually ached to see the faces of my family. So I spent one whole day hanging the pictures. I thanked God for every memory as I unpacked the box of pictures. Now I think of that wall as my wall of blessings. God is so good."

God is good. We are reassured by the knowledge that we are and always will be important to God, regardless of how our roles shift. Even as grown women, we are children of God, a God whose love strengthens and enfolds us, a God who beckons us to be the light of the world.

TRANSFORMED BY LOVE

One night when I was fighting off an overwhelming feeling of sadness, I plopped myself down on the chair in my prayer room—a small room at the back of our house, reserved for prayer. Wanting to talk to God, but unable to pray the way I wanted to, I could only muster a one-line prayer: "Lord Jesus let me feel your love."

I sat quietly in the chair, in the darkness, slowly repeating the phrase. Whenever a stray thought came into my mind, I didn't pay any attention to it. Only these words mattered: *Lord Jesus let me feel your love.*

I do not know how long I sat there praying. But a most astounding transformation took place. As I prayed, I suddenly realized that I had stopped saying, "Lord Jesus let me *feel* your love." Instead, the prayer that rose to my lips was, "Lord Jesus let me *be* your love."

I had not consciously changed the word *feel* to the word *be.* But somehow the word changed.

The realization made me sit straight up in the chair and pay attention to what the change in words meant. When I asked God to let me *feel* his love, my focus was on myself. God answered my prayer by changing my

25

words. When I asked God to let me *be* his love, the focus was outside myself. I was asking God to let me carry his love to others.

I felt my heart turning from the past to a new and hopeful future. I realized that although the emptying of my nest is inescapable and real, even more real is the immense possibility of being transformed into the love of God.

Through prayer we become better able to hear the voice of God. We learn to recognize our Creator in new people and new situations. We become adept at inwardly turning to prayer several times during the course of the day. Little by little, we will find ourselves taking on the heart and mind of Jesus Christ.

IN GOD'S PRESENCE

1) Read Isaiah 43:1-7 at bedtime. As you fall asleep, think of the infinite divine love and tenderness described in this passage.

2) The next morning, call to mind God's enormous love for you. Read the account of Jesus' baptism in Matthew 3:13-17.

3) Listen to God saying of YOU: "This is my beloved daughter. My favor rests on her." Substitute your name for the word *daughter*. Then say the passage out loud.

4) Throughout the day, call to mind the phrase: "This is my beloved daughter. My favor rests on her."

CHAPTER 2

MOM, WILL IT BE DIFFERENT WHEN I'M THE ONLY KID LEFT?

After an afternoon of helping her older brother pack for college, my daughter asked, "Mom, will it be different when I'm the only kid left?" She started to realize that the familial pattern she'd always known was about to change. No longer would she be the youngest child in a house filled with three kids. Soon she would be one of two. And then, she'd be the only child left at home.

In adjusting to our own sense of loss, it's important that we don't lose sight of the changes other family members experience. No matter how much sibling rivalry there's been, for example, children still suffer the loss of their brothers and sisters. No matter how long a younger child has been itching to have a room alone, the nights without someone to talk to are tough. Part of our continuing role as mothers is our sustained attention to our entire family.

The family dynamics don't shift all at once. Whether there is one child in a family or ten, the adjustments are gradual. It's not as if one minute there is a full house and the next moment all the bedrooms are empty. They usually get empty one at a time. Consequently, we need to stay alert to the needs of our changing families.

TRADING HEARTS WITH JESUS

To keep in touch with these changing needs, we need the patient adaptability of Jesus. One of his characteristics that continually astounds and challenges me is his infinite ability to pay attention to other people, even when he himself is exhausted and overworked. His curing of the paralytic at Capernaum, recorded in chapter 2 of Mark's Gospel, stands out as an example of this ability. Jesus apparently had returned home to Capernaum after an absence of several days, and people started to gather around the house where he stayed. The press of people was overwhelming. Four people, who were carrying a paralyzed man to Jesus, cut a hole in the roof and lowered the man down to Jesus on a mat. Mark tells us, "When Jesus saw their faith, he said to the paralyzed man, 'Son, your sins are forgiven.'"

If I sat in my living room, surrounded by scores of people, and someone cut a hole in my roof in order to lower yet another person into my house, I can think of any number of things I might say. Jesus, however, looked at the man with astounding compassion and healed him. This story of the paralytic at Capernaum pops into my head on days when my sadness over my empty house threatens to clobber my ability to pay attention to anyone else. I force myself to remember that the emptying of my house does not affect me alone. Jesus somehow always had a heart big enough to think about other people first.

Some days I just have to trade hearts with Christ, asking him to hold mine temporarily while I use his. Then, with the borrowed heart of Christ, I look again at my changing family. With Jesus' heart, my vision changes.

MANAGING THE NEW TENSIONS

Every mother faces the challenge of simultaneously adjusting her own vision, while she juggles the demands of her changing family. The changes can unleash all kinds of surprising tensions.

One of my students talked about the rage he felt when he returned home at Thanksgiving break and discovered that his sisters had turned all of his old T-shirts into car rags—and they had moved into his room! When he complained vigorously to his mom, she reassured him that he still had a place in the family. Only the "things" had changed.

As parents, we become the North Star, the fixed point against which all others are measured. And in that position, it's important to pay attention to everyone else's needs, even when those needs threaten to overwhelm us.

Marge, the mother of twelve, tried very hard to make sure that none of her younger children felt slighted as the older ones left home. This lady went to more Christmas pageants, more open houses, more bake sales than any woman I've ever known. She admitted, "After about the tenth year of seeing my kids dressed up in bathrobes, I was tempted to skip the Christmas pageants. But I couldn't let the ones still at home think that they were less important than their older brothers and sisters. The younger ones were so quick to notice a slight or a lack of attention on my part."

Perceived slights and preferential treatment always cause trouble. One of my colleagues told me—and she was serious—"If I had it to do over again, I'd only have one child. All the tension in our household comes from sibling rivalry. My husband and I never fight. But our two daughters always do. They both think the other one is the favorite, and even when they come home from college, they're at each other all the time. I hate it."

Although few of us would choose to forego mother-hood just to avoid sibling rivalry, most of us know its lethal tensions. Those tensions don't disappear in an empty nest. They just change shape.

"I cried when my oldest daughter, Janet, left home. I missed her so much," my cousin Becky explains. "But after about a week of moping around, I ran into another problem. My younger daughter got mad at me for missing her sister. 'It's not like Janet's the only kid, Mom. I'm still here.'" My cousin was bitter about her younger daughter's reaction. "I wasn't even allowed a period of mourning. Somehow missing one daughter made the other one feel slighted."

Many women echo this dilemma.

"When my oldest boy, Bobby, called to say he was coming home on leave from the Marines, I stocked the house with all his favorite foods," Nancy, a local restaurant owner, said. "I cleaned his room, bought his favorite magazines. The night he was due home, I stood in the kitchen singing to myself and making his favorite meal of stuffed cabbage. When my fifteen-year-old son, John, came home from football practice, he planted himself in front of me and said, really belligerently, 'What's the big deal about Bobby's coming home? He's not a saint or anything.'"

The great joy we feel when our children come home to visit can cause resentment. Against our will, we are cast as the prodigal mother, subject to the same familial snares that Jesus relates in the story of the prodigal son.

Dr. Lee Pattison, pastor and professor at the Jerusalem Center for Biblical Studies, talks about the parable of the prodigal son as a story of shocks. Jesus' listeners would have been shocked by the absolutely unorthodox behavior of the family in this parable. The shock of the son asking for the inheritance, the shock of the father actually giving the money to the younger son, the shock of a grown man actually running through the streets to greet his returning child. The story challenges its hearers to replace cultural expectations with compassion. Against all cultural expectations, the father responds to his son with extraordinary love.

While many families do not have to face the return of wayward children, all families have to face the inevitable clashes when the "grown and flown" siblings return and take a look at those still in the nest. Returning siblings are quick to pronounce judgment on the brothers and sisters they've left behind.

Last Christmas my older son, Tony, sized up the condition of his sister, the only one of our three children still at home. Tony looked me straight in the eye and said, "Mom, I'm going to have to drop out of college and come home just to raise this kid. It's clear you can't handle her anymore."

He was only joking. I think.

But he is not alone in his frustration. Many older children think their younger counterparts get off the hook. House rules are no longer as stringent. Parents are no longer as inflexible. The younger ones get spoiled.

Much of the grief in William Shakespeare's tragedy, *King Lear*, results from sibling rivalry. The two older daughters, Goneril and Regan, believe that their little sister, Cordelia, has always been the pet. They are all too glad to see her banished by their foolish father and all too glad to punish their father for the slights they've supposedly suffered at his hands.

Most of us are spared the tragedies that Shakespeare portrays, but every family has its own version of rivalries between grown children. Such rivalries can catch us off guard and demand mature responses from us.

One mother, with genuine embarrassment, explained a holiday incident that should have remained trivial but blossomed into a full-fledged fight. Her daughter returned home from college to discover that her younger brother had given her starter jacket to his girlfriend. This discovery was made when the parents weren't at home. By the time the parents came back, the daughter had packed her suitcase, stomped out of the house, and returned to her campus apartment.

Of course, the fight wasn't just over the starter jacket. Years of sibling rivalry triggered the larger scene. The mother was justifiably irritated that the holidays were spoiled by such an incident, but she had to dissolve her own irritation in order to calm the churning waters. We are fooling ourselves if we consider our task done when the kids leave home. We are still a family. The good things continue to bring joy, and the bad things still rankle and hurt.

Part of the resentment that older children feel is understandable. Most of us do get better at parenting the longer we're at it. So our ability to parent our younger children is better than was our ability to parent the older ones. By the time the last one reaches adolescence, we are less likely to regard every indiscretion as major. We are more flexible, more mellow.

Our older children may see our flexibility as preferential treatment, when in fact it's just plain common sense. Sometimes the firm foundation is built when we raise our older children. And the younger ones reap the benefit of our earlier firmness. Having established rules and guidelines, we can ease off a bit. What the older ones see as preferential treatment really isn't at all.

An element of petty tyranny can pop up in all of this. Georgiana, a former neighbor, told me of a predicament that caught her off guard. "My youngest child, Brittany, got very accustomed to being the only one at home. When her older sister was away at school, she didn't have to share her bedroom or bathroom or phone with anyone. When her sister came home, Brittany refused to give ground. She acted as if she was still living alone. I hadn't realized that I was allowing her to get away with more than her older sister ever did. We had to have a serious talk and lay down some new ground rules very quickly."

From the very beginning, mothers learn to respond to the varying needs and demands of their children. One toddler still needs an afternoon nap, while his four-year-old brother doesn't even know the meaning of the word *nap*. One third grader loves casseroles, while her sister refuses to touch anything but hamburgers and french fries. One teenager loves jazz, while his brother, with whom he shares a room, won't listen to anything that's not in the Top 40. Through the years, mothers learn creative ways of dealing with potential sources of friction.

That creativity is called upon again as our grown children simultaneously pull away from us and try to redefine their place in the family. Although negotiating the tricky waters may be trying at times, the negotiations are a vivid and vital reminder that we are needed still. We are mothers for life.

INVISIBLE MOTHERS

One afternoon, as I tried to pray, I was terribly distracted by memories of my early childhood, specifically of the lonely days when my older sister started first grade, leaving me alone. For some reason, I decided to indulge this distraction instead of fighting it. I asked God to help me view my childhood loneliness. And do you know what God showed me? I wasn't alone. My mother was there—unseen, unheard, but there.

Almost as if the Holy Spirit were nudging me from memory to memory, I gratefully remembered all the activities of those days. I thought of my mother watching me rollerskate on the newly tarred street, and helping me gather twigs of ivy to build into make-believe fires. She was the one who suggested that I rake leaves for the elderly couple across the street. And she gave me an old blanket to cover the bed of pine needles that gathered under the enormous pine tree in our front yard—the blanket let me play under the tree without getting stuck with the sharp needles.

Then, I vividly remember my mother taking me with her as we walked to pick up my sister from school. She didn't leave me at a neighbor's house, because she knew that I'd feel better seeing where my sister was. Certainly my mother was experiencing her own sense of loss. Her first child had started school. But she did what she could to make the change easier for me.

None of these memories were new. Through the years I've often thought about the skates, the leaves, the ivy, and the pine tree. But after asking God to help me view the events, I gained something new. This prayer experience heightened my gratitude for my own mother. And it made me realize how important our very presence is to our changing families.

As a small child, I was unaware of my mother's pain in sending my sister off to school, and I was largely oblivious to her efforts to ease my loneliness. Only as an adult, looking back with the help of the Holy Spirit, was I able to discern that my mother's presence made all the difference in the world. And, of course, in my current situation, where I feel increasingly invisible as a mother, this insight from the Holy Spirit seems like a precious gift.

Many of our maternal efforts are not grandiose ones. As we weave and bob, trying to cope with the pressures of our grown-up families, even those closest to us will be unaware of our efforts. But our efforts stand, nonetheless. My mother's loving presence was no less real just because as a small child I was largely unaware of her attempts to care for me.

Raising our own children makes most of us ever more appreciative of our mothers. We gain strength and comfort from knowing that our own moms—and millions of women like them—have successfully faced the challenges of motherhood. We know that, at every stage, mothering calls forth the best from us. With each new phase, God invites us to find new ways to love. Changes may be temporarily unsettling, but they offer such possibilities for growth. As Christian mothers, Easter is at the center of our faith and our lives. With our eyes on the Resurrected Lord, we can openly embrace our changing roles.

IN GOD'S PRESENCE

1) As you acknowledge Christ's presence, leaf through a family photo album of your children's early years: their birthday parties or Christmas celebrations or first days of school.

2) When a particular event catches your attention, allow yourself to remember the event: How old were you at the time? How old was your child? What were you wearing? What kind of day was it?

3) Ask Christ to remind you of the good you accomplished that day. Don't rush this part of the prayer. Let yourself be reminded of your goodness.

4) Offer a silent prayer of thanksgiving to Christ for all the opportunities he's given you to carry out his will.

CHAPTER 3

MOTHER FOR LIFE

After the opening night performance of the fall play, *A Man for All Seasons*, the student cast and their families began the short walk from the theater to the reception. Dressed in their Renaissance costumes, the students looked like a vision of the sixteenth century as they walked across the campus in the cool November air.

Shortly after we started, the young man who played Thomas More stopped and looked up. "Hey," he yelled to no one in particular, "I lost my mom." The long, velvet-trimmed cape he wore whirled around him as he scanned the group for his mother.

The image pressed into my memory.

Twenty minutes earlier this student had brought a crowd of 900 people to its feet as they gave him a standing ovation for his portrayal of Thomas More. Now suddenly, here he was, a son who'd "lost his mom."

We may be tempted to believe that our children don't need us anymore after they leave home. In that first flurry of their packing up and moving away, we feel lost. We don't have to cook for them, do their laundry, or listen to them. But the reality is that our children always need us.

STILL LOVED AND NEEDED

On a recent trip to Israel, my husband and I met an eighty-year-old mother who was traveling with her

sixty-year-old daughter. The whole tour group was solic-
itous of the older woman's health, fearful that the
relentless pace of the trip would prove too much for her.
One day when mother and daughter failed to show up
for our morning departure, we all assumed the mother
was ill and the daughter had stayed to care for her. But
no. It was the other way around. The daughter was ill,
and the mother stayed with her.

The next day the eighty-year-old mom announced
cheerily, "Well, no one ever said you are only a mother
for twenty years!"

When my husband and I returned from this trip, I was
curious to know how our sixteen-year-old daughter had
fared. We'd left her with some friends of ours who
absolutely cherish her, so we knew she'd been in good
hands. When I asked her how she'd survived in our
absence, she said, "Well, Mom, it was a different two
weeks. I'll give you that. I was okay. I mean I know how
to do my own laundry and cook and stuff. But it was
like the little pillow was gone."

The little pillow was gone. I like the sound of those
words. The days of our daughter's total dependence on
us no longer exist. Clearly, she can survive, even when
we are thousands of miles away. Still, as parents we
form a vital link—a little pillow—in her existence that
no one else can fill. Even after she leaves home, we will
still be that vital link. We don't abdicate our responsibilities as the children leave home. They still need us.

Thinking of our own parents drives this point home.
My father and mother are still vitally important in my
life. My father continues to be the wisest man I've ever
known. His advice is always crucial to me. I have never
yet made a major decision without seeking his counsel.
My friends call me with their own problems and ask,
"What would your dad say about this?" And my mother's

seemingly boundless love sustains me. My mother wouldn't disown me even if I decided to join a band of wandering gypsies. She still worries about me, prays for me, and occasionally cooks for me. I still need her.

Right before Easter last year my mother sent me a note explaining that one of her coworkers had shown her the Easter dresses she purchased for her little daughters. My mother wrote: "The little dresses she bought are white with navy blue trim, and they have little hats to match and little sticky-outy petticoats. For some reason when she pulled those two dresses out of the bag, I got all choked up, remembering how many Easter dresses I shopped for when you girls were little."

My mom still gets teary thinking about buying dresses for me and my sisters, even though we are decades past that stage. Who else in the whole world is ever going to have fond memories of buying me a little dress? I may have left home twenty-five years ago, but my parents never left me. They are always within reach.

The longing for steadfast and loving parents is a universal one.

How often I wish that the parents of my students could hear their children talking about them. One day, shortly before spring break, a student appeared in my office doorway. In his dress uniform, with medals and insignia on his chest, he plopped down dejectedly in a chair. When I asked him what was wrong, out came a steady stream of misery. "My girlfriend says she wants to date other guys. My history prof just told me I got a D on the midterm. My stupid car needs $200 worth of repairs again."

He talked for about ten minutes; then, he said, "Yeah, so I called my mom last night, and I'm going home for spring break." In talking to his mother, this young man realized that all he wanted to do was go home. Previously, he'd made plans to spend spring break in Florida with some friends. But he was so worn out, so down in the dumps, that he knew he simply had to go home.

Implicit in his behavior and his emotions was the knowledge that his mom, although she couldn't remedy everything, loved him. He could go home, sleep in his own bed, hang around the house in an old pair of sweats, be around someone who was grateful just to be near him. And he knew his mom waited for him with love.

Mothering sometimes carries us very close to the heart of God.

David, another student, made a lasting impression on me in this regard. Once he mentioned in passing that he'd gone home with a friend the night before. The friend complained all night long about his nagging mother, even snidely mimicking her constant admonitions: "Wear a sweater. It's cold. Make sure there's gas in your car. Don't forget to let the car warm up."

David looked at me and said, "My mother died when I was three. I wish I had somebody who told me to put on a sweater. My friend doesn't know how lucky he is to have a mother."

David didn't want a perfect mother. He simply wanted a mother. He needed a mother.

My neighbor, Betty, went to a funeral for a woman in her early forties who died of leukemia. Betty called me in tears and said, "Oh, you should have seen her poor daughters. They need their mother so much." Both daughters are grown and in college. Of course they need their mother.

Motherhood is not negated because we are no longer the ones who pick our children up after play practice, because we are no longer the ones to call the school when they are sick and cannot attend class, because we no longer know every piece of clothing in their wardrobes. Our grown children still love and need us.

STAYING CONNECTED

Mary, the mother of Jesus, did not cease to be part of her son's life when he left home. In fact, she was a part of his ministry. In the second chapter of John's Gospel, the writer recounts the miracle at Cana. It is Mary who turns to her son and says, "They have no more wine." And although Christ seems at first reluctant to act, telling his mother, "My time has not yet come," his mother knows he will respond to her concern. Mary tells the servants, "Do whatever he tells you." And the water is transformed into wine.

Jesus' treatment of his mother has always baffled and bothered me. More than once in the Gospel, he seems to dismiss her—in ways that must have wounded her. After three anxious days of searching, Mary and Joseph find Jesus in the Temple and Jesus tells his mother, "Why were you searching for me? Didn't you know I had to be in my Father's house?" Later, in his adult ministry, as Luke tells us in chapter 8 of his Gospel, Jesus' "mother and brothers came to see him, but they were not able to get near him because of the crowd." How does Jesus respond? He says, "My mother and brothers are those who hear God's word and put it into practice." Even if Mary understood her son's ministry, these words must have bothered her. And from the cross when Jesus sees Mary with his beloved John, he gives her away, saying of John, "Dear woman, here is your son." While the words may well be ones of compassion for his suffering mother, Mary must have felt a sword piercing her heart.

Certainly, Mary suffered when her son left home. After all, he must have left quite an empty place at the dinner table! Yet despite her own painful adjustments and other family responsibilities, and despite her son's sometimes baffling treatment of her, she remained available to her grown son until the horrible end.

Our connections to our grown children may not be as dramatic as Mary's. Nonetheless, our gracious adjustment to changing relationships with our children is vital.

During his freshman year at college, my son developed a throat infection that required medical attention. The campus health center prescribed some pills. And in his usual off-handed way, my son was taking them. Wanting to know the name of the medication and the results of his throat culture, I phoned the health center from my office and asked the nurse for the information.

"We cannot give out that information to anyone," the nurse said.

Thinking I must have forgotten to identify myself, I told the woman, "Oh, I'm his mother. You can tell me."

The nurse replied, "Your son is 18. By law we cannot disclose health information to anyone but him."

I'm not sure if my frustration or fury was greater. If my son were home, our physician wouldn't hesitate to talk to me. I would have been the one to take him to the doctor, to pick up (and pay for!) the medication. But because he had left home, his physical condition was no longer my business.

The stunning reality made me miserable. I felt as if my role as the monitor of my son's health had been wrested from me by some anonymous, health-center nurse who didn't care about my son's throat any more than she cared about anyone else's. At that moment, I did not feel like graciously responding to my changing role in my son's life.

As I sat at my desk feeling grumpy, a student wandered in to talk about an essay assignment. Although he clearly needed extra help, he fidgeted in the chair. Finally, he stood up abruptly, announcing, "Gotta go check my mail. I'm hoping my Easter basket comes today."

"Easter basket?" I asked.

"Yeah, my mom better send me one. She always made me one when I was at home."

I was stunned. This freshman in college, eighteen years old, easily over six feet tall, was expecting an Easter basket from his mom. Perhaps his mother couldn't get the results of his throat culture either, but she could still give him an Easter basket.

Our children do expect us to maintain traditions and connections: Keep their Christmas stockings on the mantel. Send care packages. Provide airline tickets home. Care about them when they're ill.

When my son had his four wisdom teeth removed last year, I drove to Cleveland. Granted he had a whole slew of aunts and grandparents and friends who could have taken care of him, but I did not want my son put under general anesthesia while I sat, worrying, in Maryland. Right until the moment he lost consciousness my son kept telling me, "You didn't have to come here for this. It's a waste of time."

But after the teeth were pulled and he regained consciousness, only to feel that sickening reel of nausea brought on by the anesthetic and blood-drenched saliva, the poor kid looked at me and mouthed the words, "I'm glad you're here."

Over the next few days, as I stayed with him at my mom's, making sure he took the antibiotics and pain pills every four hours, I realized how deeply I missed his company. Even sick and woozy, this child was a good companion. His leaving home—his leaving me—left a hole in my existence. I was glad to have the chance to be of some use to him again.

The needs of our grown children may not be immediately evident to us. On a daily basis, as we pursue lives without them, we may be unaware that our very existence matters to them. Our voice at the other end of the phone when they call; our congratulations when they land a new job; our sympathy when they fail a course—all are important. We will always be the ones who remember our children at the moment of birth. We will carry with us images of their first school play, their first bicycles, their first dates. When they reminisce about their childhoods, they count on us to share their memories.

Babies needing bottles and toddlers needing Band-Aids were easy to help. All of us learned quickly to set up a Kool-Aid stand on summer days when our offspring suddenly turned entrepreneurial! Most of us, more than once, produced a batch of cookies overnight when given only last-minute warning of a bake sale. Now, the demands of our children will not be so obvious.

Another opportunity of the empty nest is the chance to fine-tune our vision and develop keener powers of observation. Our children will no longer turn to us for help memorizing multiplication tables. But turn to us, they will. And we need to be there, alert to all the silent signals, when they do.

THEY DO NOT BELONG TO US

Most of us will gladly continue to be of use to our children. We maintain traditions and connections. Our children also need to see us moving on with our lives, however, staying alive, not stagnating. We keep praying, and we keep going. The saddest parents are those whose lives really do stop when their children leave home, the ones who cannot carry themselves past the loss of their children and who get mired in self-pity.

A church member, Regina, tells an almost unbelievable tale about her own mother, a mother who never adjusted to the empty nest. After her mother died, Regina and her brothers went to the bank to clear out their mom's safety deposit box. There in a brown enve-

44

lope addressed to the children was a letter from their mother. She intended for them to read it after her death.

In her own handwriting, Regina's mother talked about what a joy the children had been to raise. She spoke lovingly of those cherished years when they lived with her. The letter, however, went on to say that when her children left home, she became miserable and despondent. Her empty nest made her bitter and unhappy.

"I never got over your leaving me," this woman wrote. "My life was over once you kids were gone."

Columnist Ellen Goodman discusses the tough procedure of learning to let go. "What I have learned," Goodman writes, "is that our children may be our own but we can't claim ownership. What I have learned is that . . . we must learn to share children. We share them with the world. But most particularly, we learn to share them with themselves."

One of my students talked about his mother's response to a whopping mistake he'd made. "You know she was really good about my screw-up," this young man told me. "She didn't yell or cry or anything. All she said was that she and Dad were disappointed. And then she said, 'We can't make you us.'"

The wisdom of that mother's line—"We can't make you us"—jumped out at me. I'll probably never meet this woman, but her approach to parenting a grown child seems particularly appropriate to me. Our children are separate from us.

They are not ours. We do not own them. We never did. Kahlil Gibran, in *The Prophet*, makes this point so clearly. Of our children Gibran says: ". . . though they are with you, yet they belong not to you. You may give them your love but not your thoughts. For they have their own thoughts. You may house their bodies but not their souls."

45

When children leave home, we can grow sad, even truly despondent. Their leaving shocks and surprises us. One minute it seems they are omnipresent, depending on us for every need. The next minute they're loading the van with their clothes and books. For decades, our children are woven into every decision, every trip, every dinner. Then, poof, only their graduation pictures greet us when we climb the stairs at night. Missing our children is part of loving them. But part of loving them is letting our lives continue after they have left us.

SETTING AN EXAMPLE

More than ever, I realize that the example I set for my kids is crucial. My oldest son called home on a Sunday afternoon and said, "So, did you sleep in this morning, Mom?" I laughed at him and said, "You know I was in church." Quick as only he can be, Tony replied, "Oh, now that we're not around, you don't have to keep going to church."

We both knew he was teasing. But should I ever stop going to church, should my prayer life dry up, should I turn my back on Jesus Christ, my children would be the first to notice. And they would be hurt by my turning away. True, most of the time they're not around to attend church with me anymore. If I stopped attending, however, they would feel the impact.

William Bennett in his book, *The Book of Virtues*, records a tale called "Grandmother's Table." Adapted from the Brothers Grimm, the short piece recounts the story of a feeble, old widow who was forced to live with her son and his wife and daughter. Because the old woman's table manners were horrible—she spilled a glass of milk, dropped her peas—the husband and his wife made her sit at a small table in the corner and eat by herself. That way they wouldn't have to suffer her miserable eating habits. Then, so the story goes, "One evening just before dinner [the daughter] was busy playing on the floor with her building blocks, and her father asked her what she was making. 'I'm building a little table for you and mother,' she smiled, 'so you can eat by yourselves in the corner someday when I get big.'"

The tale sternly reminds us that our children always watch us. When they are grown, our example remains important.

My mother-in-law, Ruth, demonstrated the importance of setting an example for grown children. When her children left home, she was well into her sixties, and she continued to serve God and the church. If ever a woman embodied Proverbs 31:10-31, it was Ruth Wintermute Drew. In many ways, my husband gained the most from his parents when he left home. As a child, he felt discomfort over having "fuddy-duddy" older parents. As an adult, he came to realize what extraordinary people they were. The example they set—as God-loving, church-going, forward-looking people—continued to be an inspiration long after he left home.

One day, not long before her death, I was talking to Ruth about this book, and my husband was in the room. He asked his mom, in all seriousness, "Did you miss me when I left for college?"

Ruth looked rather hurt, as she said, "Of course I missed you. We dropped you off at college, and then I didn't get to see you again until Thanksgiving. It was very hard on me."

Until that moment, it had never occurred to my husband that his mother suffered when he left home. She never mentioned it. Her busy and active life continued after her nest was empty. As parents, we are our children's first teachers. We teach them the value of life and of God. We are diminished when they leave home. We are saddened, perhaps indulging in a good cry when we stand in their empty bedrooms. But, we are not just their first teachers, we are their lifelong teachers. Even when they are beyond the reach of our arms, we want them to see in us the love of God.

Our children should know that we miss them. However, they should also know, by our example, that life is a continual weaving together of threads and pieces. God was good enough to give us our children.. And we have to be good enough to let them go.

One summer when I was lucky enough to be in England, I went walking in Thornthwaite Forest in the Lake District. If there is a more beautiful spot on earth, I have not seen it. All alone, I talked to God and wandered over soft beds of pine needles. I was actually singing by the time I found a clearing from where I could see the shining Lake Bassenthwaite below—singing because I felt so grateful to be alive, grateful for my life, and oh! so glad to be in England.

My older son came to mind. The world, as it stretched out before me, seemed so shining, so full of possibilities. And I thought with real longing of the little boy who had grown into an extraordinary young man, with a unique set of talents and graces. There in the forest, overlooking Lake Bassenthwaite, I realized that my son was grown and that never again would I plop him in the car seat for a long ride to see his grandmother. Never again would I sew patches on his Boy Scout uniform. Never again would I cheer him on as he came to bat.

As I thought about the little boy who had grown, I wondered, in God's presence, what there was left for me to do. And if God has ever spoken to me, it was then. What God said was this: *You can tell Tony that life is good. And love is endless. And although there is great grief in the world, there is much good to be done. Then you can live a life that proves all this to be true.*

When I finally meet God and express thanks for the many blessings of my life, high on my list of blessings will be this message from Lake Bassenthwaite. Because it was there I learned that my own life well-lived is its own answer to the empty nest.

———

IN GOD'S PRESENCE

1) At bedtime, read John 2:1-11—the wedding at Cana. Think about the passage as you fall asleep.

2) The next morning, before your day begins, reread the passage as if you were a guest at the wedding. Imagine that you are a friend of Mary's with grown children of your own. How must Mary have felt? How would her friends and family have reacted before and after the miracle? Can we learn anything from watching this exchange between Mary and her grown son?

3) Offer a silent prayer, thanking God for giving us this scripture passage.

4) Throughout the day, call to mind the mature relationship of Jesus and his mother.

CHAPTER 4

WHAT ARE WE SUPPOSED TO DO NOW THAT THE KIDS ARE GONE?

In trying to help a group of college freshmen understand the pangs that their parents might be going through, an academic dean, who has been happily married three decades, confessed, "My last daughter left for college today. That means tomorrow morning, when I'm eating my bran muffin and drinking my orange juice, I'll be eating breakfast alone with my wife for the first time in almost thirty years. That terrifies me."

This man loved his wife—really loved her. But his life was about to change. The dean was a little nervous.

Even the strongest of couples worry about the inevitable changes that come with the empty nest. Mary, a farmer's wife of thirty years, said, "Remember that horrible scene in *Gone With the Wind* when Bonnie dies? Well, it's after that pretty little girl dies that Rhett leaves Scarlett. He just tells her that as long as their daughter was alive, there was hope for the two of them. With the baby gone, he can't stay with Scarlett. I always kind of worried that my husband might be a little like that. He was so partial to our girls—we had five of them—that I was afraid that once it was just me and him, he'd want to leave. But he's still here. And they've all been gone a long time now. So I guess I'm safe."

Mary and her husband seem like the salt of the earth, warmhearted, decent, God-filled people who have a large brood of children and grandchildren. Never would I have guessed that Mary harbored fears about her marriage. But she did. She feared that her husband's attachment to the children was greater than his attachment to her.

After talking to Mary, I asked an old friend if the thought of her impending empty nest made her apprehensive about her marriage. Without hesitation, she responded brightly, "Heavens no! My husband and I like each other."

Her quick and emphatic response gave me cause to wonder. Oh, I know that she and her husband are well-matched and have been happier than most couples. However, all change carries with it apprehension. Maybe we don't all share Mary's fear that our husbands will depart once the children are gone. Just the same, human beings wonder how change will affect them. We wonder how the arrival of that first baby will alter our lives, and we wonder how the departures will affect our relationship with our spouse.

NEW OPPORTUNITIES

Many women are joyously surprised by the improvement in their marriages as the children leave.

Margaret, a library aide, talked about the reduction of domestic tension. "I never thought of our house as a tense one," this mother of three recounts. "But when our oldest son left home, you could almost feel the house breathe a little easier. Then when the other two left, the house let out an enormous sigh of relief."

Lizzie, a friend of my mother's, echoed this sentiment. "It's not like my husband and I stopped being good buddies when the kids were born. But kids are so all-consuming and demanding. Maybe I shouldn't say this, but I'm glad they're finally gone. Jim and I have more time for each other."

Even Grace, a woman who'd been lucky enough to have a live-in maid when her son was small, found the freedom of the empty nest to be a real asset. "I always went with my husband on his business trips and for short little getaways when my boy was little. So I never felt trapped. But when our son left home, I was relieved that my husband and I could travel and not worry about childcare arrangements."

Sometimes we don't realize the tensions brought on by the routine tasks of making a house run smoothly. Once parts of the puzzle are removed, there is a sense of relief. And the couple is the beneficiary.

Agnes, a woman in her seventies, grinned when asked about the years when her children left home. "You know," she said, blushing a bit and having trouble getting the words out, "you know, your husband and you can goof around more without all those kids around all the time." And we both knew what she meant by "goof around."

Perhaps part of the reason that children have always seen their parents as asexual beings is because having kids in every corner of a house can seriously hamper even the most romantic of impulses! Once a couple no longer has to worry about a face unexpectedly appearing in the bedroom doorway, there is more opportunity to "goof around," as Agnes put it. The character Vinnie on the television show "Doogie Howser" told Doogie's parents when their son was leaving home, "Hey! Remember. Every room is now a bedroom." The grin on his face matched Agnes'.

Enormous advantages present themselves to couples, if they stay open and flexible. Although the financial

Marriage is, as the wedding ceremony reminds us, "a school of perfection, a sign of Christ's redeeming love." Our spouses are companions for the journey to God.

Robert Browning's touching poem expresses the promise of this journey. "Grow old along with me, the best is yet to be—the last of life for which the first is made." How odd those words sounded when we were in our twenties, but now with a few decades under our belts, our perspective changes. Everything we've experienced in our lives up to this point makes us ready to embrace the next phase. Thanks in large part to the workings of grace, the passing years have strengthened us and made us more resilient. That strength and resilience will serve us well as we and our spouse throw our hearts into the future.

Almost every human being I've ever known very well longs to feel singularly precious and treasured in someone's eyes. Indifference, even malice, at the hands of other people are bearable, if we know that there is reserved for us alone a place where we are cherished above all others. Some of my closest friends have sacrificed almost everything in order to stay near a source of such love.

As mothers, most of us know how to love our children. As wives, we may have to be reminded how to love our husbands. Without the endless demands of the kids, perhaps we can funnel some of our energy toward our mates, creating for them a place of being cherished. These haunting lines from the Song of Songs remind me of the fierce and eternal love found in vital marriages:

> Place me like a seal over your heart,
>   like a seal over your arm;
> for love is as strong as death,
>   its jealousy unyielding as the grave.
> It burns like blazing fire,
>   like a mighty flame (8:6).

SURVIVING THE EMPTY NEST DETOURS

While many women are surprised by the joy of having more time to spend with their spouses, many are also acutely aware that men, at the empty nest stage, often must steer through their own set of detours, to use the phrase James A. Harnish coins in his book *Men at Mid-Life*. These detours can undermine a marriage.

"I'm holding on to hope. That's all," Catherine announced to her prayer group, "hope that Ralph will snap out of his slump." Ralph, her machinist husband, had grown despondent when the kids left home. "Sometimes I'll see him flipping through old photo albums, crying. But the funny thing is, he's not looking at pictures of the kids when they were younger. He's looking at pictures of himself."

We've all read about the midlife crises of men. How often as kids growing up did we hear that horrible joke about a middle-aged man trading in his forty-year-old wife for two "twenties"? Now that we've reached middle-age, the joke is still horrible, but we can see it acted out all around us.

A woman, whose name I don't even know, tearfully told me about her husband's leaving her for his twenty-three-year-old secretary. We were both sitting in a college bookstore, waiting for our freshman sons to get through an enormously long checkout line with their books. We started chatting about how tough it was to have children leave home. Suddenly this woman was in tears, as she told me about it: "And my husband left me last year. He moved in with his twenty-three-year-old secretary. So now there's nobody at home. I don't have a husband or kids. My whole life is supposed to be ahead of me. But what's the point?"

I can picture her so clearly, sitting in a hard-backed, black chair, staring at her son in the long cashier's line. She wasn't talking to me as much as she was uttering her words into space. "My whole life is supposed to be ahead of me. But what's the point?" This woman faced enormous adjustments, brought on in large measure by her husband's own midlife crisis.

The myth of the middle-aged man abandoning his family, buying a red sports car, and taking off with his secretary may be exaggerated, but like all myths it arises from the impulses of life. Like all the stages of life, middle age has its potential potholes. Being aware of them is the first step in avoiding them.

A silly football game made me realize the changes my own husband was facing. As I headed upstairs one Monday night to grade a batch of essays, I glanced into the family room. There was my husband watching "Monday Night Football"—alone.

It suddenly struck me how hard that must be for him. From the time they were very small, our sons used to watch the games with him. As the boys got older, they'd tell their dad about the game on those nights when a church meeting made him miss a broadcast. Now, my husband watched the games alone, with only an occasional visit from me. The loss of the boys' companionship was no small matter.

Just as our children leave home, our husbands face the decline and death of their own parents. They may face a plateau in their professional lives. Their girth may spread into that miserable, middle-aged affliction known as a "potbelly." Their hair may turn gray or fall out. Their word may no longer carry the authority it once did.

These kinds of potholes affect marriages.

Jacklyn, a red-haired woman in her fifties, discovered one such pothole only gradually. After her oldest son left home, Jacklyn had expected things to improve around the house. Her husband and son had always been at odds, often bickered, and sometimes yelled at each other. The father developed a history of berating the son, picking at him over little faults, real and imagined. At first, the tension subsided when the boy left home. Then little by little, Jacklyn noticed a disturbing trend. Her husband started berating her, as he had once berated their son.

When she called this emotional pattern to her husband's attention, he told her she was imagining things. But she wasn't. The way she ate her cereal, the way she sat in her chair, the way she started the car, the way she opened her bills—normal activities became a source of insidious tension, as her husband commented on everything she did. Having grown accustomed to having someone around to ridicule, he now used his wife as the scapegoat.

"It drove me batty," Jacklyn admits. "But the solution was so simple, it almost makes me laugh—although at the time I was ready to kill him. For one week, I made a list of every negative thing my husband said to me. Then I made a tape of the list. In my normal voice, I just read all the stuff onto the tape. One day before leaving for work, I put the tape in his car, ready to start as soon as he turned the key."

When she came home from work that night, her husband sat at the kitchen table, slowly pulling the magnetic tape from the cassette. After he finished, he knotted the tape into a ball and threw it in the wastebasket.

"That's the last you'll hear of that garbage," her husband told her.

This couple never talked about the incident, never went to counseling. They handled one of their empty-nest problems in a unique way—the way that worked for them. What strikes me about the particular adjustment Larry and Jacklyn made is that the problem was an unexpected one. It wasn't one they would have anticipated as they envisioned the snares the empty nest might hold.

Cleo, a grandmother of ten, explained a surprise that the empty nest tossed at her. "I always assumed," Cleo said, "that when the kids left, my husband and I would pick up right where we left off, back before we had kids. But we couldn't. The years had changed us. All those years we had our marriage on the back burner, I guess. Now, in a way, I feel like we're starting from scratch."

Many couples are able, like Cleo and her husband, to "start from scratch"—to get to know and love each other all over again. Yet there are those couples who— sometimes despite their best efforts—find the detours only lead to a dead end.

When my lifelong friend, Cathie, called from Arizona to tell me that her divorce was final, she said, "It took the kids leaving home for me to realize how miserable my marriage was. I've apologized to God, but I have more than half of my life still ahead of me. I just don't want to be miserable anymore."

Married to a successful lawyer, Cathie raised the couple's two children. In order to build his law practice, her husband joined the Kiwanis and several civic and business organizations. He played pickup basketball on Wednesday and Friday nights. He golfed on Saturdays. When the rest of the family went to church on Sunday mornings, he went to the country club for brunch. Whenever Cathie begged, pleaded even, with him to make more time for the family, he would say, "Everything I do is for the family. I'm working to give us a good life."

But Cathie knew better.

Over the years, she'd call me, sobbing, in sheer frustration. "Pray for me," she'd say. "I'm not going to make it." For twenty-five years she put up with the loneliness and the anguish because of the children. She became involved in her children's schools, an exercise program, the church. A gracious companion at the many social events they attended, Cathie, like many women, learned to make the best of a bad situation.

Then one by one her children started to leave.

And when her husband was gone every day of the week, she was alone. The children seemed to no longer need her. And she had to reexamine her own life. She went to a counselor who, after a few weeks of talking to Cathie, asked to see her husband. Her husband repeatedly refused, saying: "You're the only one having problems. I'm fine." Cathie decided to leave.

The empty nest made her realize that she'd only been able to endure the pain because of the children. But they were gone, living their own lives, as they should be.

Cathie's not alone, of course. Many couples reexamine the trouble spots once the house is devoid of offspring. And some couples are forced to face the painful truth: Only the children kept the marriage intact. Once the door closes on the last child, the marriage looks lifeless.

Both the Old and New Testaments uphold the sanctity of marriage, reminding us that "marriage should be honored by all" (Hebrews 13:4*a*). However, more than one writer in the Bible acknowledges the tugs and pulls that can create domestic troubles. The tugging and pulling, the tensions, can make us incapable of living out Christ's commandment: "Love each other as I have loved you" (John 15:12).

In discussing those tugs and pulls, a Christian radio show host talked about marriages that get killed on the "altar of activity." Such marriages are eaten away, as if by termites, when husband and wife will not slow down and pay attention to each other. When warmth and tenderness are replaced by excessive meetings and endless business trips, we can easily allow the devil to pollute our understanding of God's will. And by the time we realize what has happened, which is often only when the kids leave home, the damage done by termites is pretty far advanced.

No person of faith embraces divorce as an ultimate good; however, we cannot ignore the reality that some relationships cannot be salvaged. Sometimes we must rely on the ultimate mercy of God, accept divine forgiveness, and reach for new life.

THE BEST NEWS

The empty nest brings change, to be sure—change that can affect the marriage relationship positively or negatively. The good news is that most couples do survive the adjustments and detours, often finding their empty nest years to be the most fulfilling of their married life. The key is to focus on the possibilities and new opportunities.

Cleo, the same grandmother of ten who talked about starting over from scratch, reached for her Bible as she talked to me. "Listen to this," she said: "For the wedding of the Lamb has come, and his bride has made herself ready. Fine linen, bright and clean, was given her to wear" (Rev. 19:7b-8). At first I didn't see the connection she was making. Then she explained: When John talks about how the resurrected church will be, how the second coming will be, he talks about a wedding and a bride. When he wants to talk about great joy, he mentions a wedding. Isn't that the best news?"

Well, yes, it is the best news. Marriage carries with it all the hope of the resurrection and eternal life. Our courage and steadfastness in the face of empty nest detours can remain constant if we remember the words of Paul to the Romans: "For I am convinced that neither death nor life, neither angels nor demons, neither the present nor the future, nor any powers, neither height nor depth, nor anything else in all creation, will be able to separate us from the love of God that is in Christ Jesus our Lord" (8:38-39).

———

IN GOD'S PRESENCE

1) In the morning read 1 Corinthians 13.

2) Then read the first part of 1 Corinthians 14.

3) Choose one part of Paul's description of love in 1 Corinthians 13 and aim to show your spouse that kind of love today.

4) Throughout the day, remember that Paul suggests that true love is our aim, our goal. It does not happen all at once.

CHAPTER 5

IF ONLY I COULD START OVER AGAIN KNOWING WHAT I KNOW NOW

There are crystal clear moments that I remember from each of my children's initial days on this earth. My oldest son Tony's first afternoon at home provides me with such a memory. The newborn baby was, I thought, asleep in his cradle. Lying in a position that is characteristic of the way he sleeps even now—face to the left, on his stomach, both arms down at his sides—his breathing was quiet and small. As I crossed from the kitchen to the bedroom in our small apartment, I glanced through the bars of his wooden cradle—only to be startled by Tony's wide-open eyes. His big eyes with those stunningly dark lashes stared out from under the crocheted afghan. Here was a brand new person, fresh from God, looking quietly at the world.

Even now I can close my own eyes and see that new little person looking out from under the blanket. And I wish the rewind button worked for parenting. If only with the wisdom I've gained in the past twenty years, I could now raise my son. But as my own father tells me, "That's not how it works. You learn how to be a parent by doing it. You're bound to make mistakes."

Still, I sometimes wish I could find the little people that my children used to be—and try again.

WE ALL MAKE MISTAKES

In his novel *David Copperfield* Charles Dickens provides an account of a loving mother who made a grievous error. When young David returns from boarding school to find his beloved mother unexpectedly remarried to the menacing Mr. Murdstone, he feels as if his whole world has been stripped away from him. Desperate for some word of comfort or reassurance, the little boy, with a tear-streaked face, stands in the family parlor, longing for his mother to embrace and reassure him. She does not move. Remembering these forlorn moments as an adult, David writes: "God help me, I might have been improved for my whole life . . . by a kind word at that season . . . a word of welcome home, of reassurance that it was home . . . but the word was not spoken and the time for it was gone."

That phrase—*the word was not spoken and the time for it was gone*—resounds inside my head sometimes. Like David's well-intentioned but weak mother, we all make mistakes in judgment.

In years past, when I imagined what I might come to regret about my child-raising years, I developed a long list of possibilities. Some were trivial, others far less so. Maybe I didn't pay enough attention to all of their tears. Maybe purchasing rather than making Halloween costumes was a mistake. (I knew a mother who linked thousands of paper clips together to make her son a medieval coat of mail.) Abandoning my Grandma Ilacqua's recipe for spaghetti sauce in favor of Ragu was not a good thing. And, of course, I did wonder if my decision to pursue my own career would seem like a mistake in retrospect.

Now that my children are grown, none of those

things bothers me. What I wish more than anything is that, in the early years, our home had been a kinder one. Softer. Let me explain.

When my children were very small, my husband was struggling to establish himself in his first full-time church. My husband's youthfulness, among other things, disgruntled some church members. The church had expected an older pastor, one who wasn't still wet behind the ears. In his youthful inexperience and insecurity, my husband set out to prove that he was worthy of his congregation's respect. Along the way, he did a lot of good.

In addition to his routine pastoral duties, he started a Senior Ministries program, a Meals-on-Wheels program, and a day care center. He joined the area civic club and was appointed to the community development committee and the regional mental health board. He started a healing ministry and began private counseling sessions with church members. During the summers, he gathered up the youth to work on Appalachian Service Projects. So outstanding were his efforts, he received special recognition from the mayor and city council.

Night after night, week after week, month after month, my husband worked very hard. And I sat home alone, first with one child, then with two, then with three. The complicated birth of our second son depleted my physical stamina. And by the time I had to face major surgery after the birth of our third child, my endurance was at an all-time low. During these difficult times, the demands of the church did not abate.

I was not gracious. I raged.

My husband insisted adamantly that he was merely doing God's work. I, even more vehemently, insisted that God never demands that we behave in ways that consistently distort the natural order of charity. My husband, after all, did have a wife and family. The grief in our household grew, as too many people, for their own reasons, tried to take advantage of the tensions between my husband and me. Looking back now, I feel certain that Satan was throttling us with both of his hands.

Inevitably my own children, the munchkins, could not help but absorb the tension in the house. That little baby who looked out from under the blanket, wondering what the world might be like, learned a pretty rough lesson. Sometimes the world is a place filled with the sounds of your mother sobbing, your parents arguing, and the slamming of doors.

I prayed, hard, through all the turmoil. "Grant me, O Lord, a heart strong enough to endure the struggle." My prayers, feeble as they were, sustained me. But the strain was nearly soul-breaking. I regret, not only for my sake but also for the sake of my children, that I did not learn quickly enough how to handle the pain and sadness when the early years of marriage turned out to be so difficult.

An almost endless list of misgivings emerges when mothers are asked about what mistakes they might have made. One thing that struck me in my conversations with women is the number of mothers who blamed themselves for being too lenient. One woman said, "I think maybe I wasn't firm enough with them. I let them get away with too much." Another sighed and announced, "They weren't ready for the real world. I did everything for them."

One woman thinks her leniency grew from her son's premature birth. She always thought of his health as fragile, so she never let him do anything for himself and never wanted to upset him. She avoided disagreements at all costs. Another mother, with an epileptic daughter, believes that it was her daughter's medical condition that made her overly pliable. Because the daughter couldn't get a driver's license, the mother accompanied her everywhere. Fearing that emotional stress would trigger a seizure, this mother allowed her daughter to have her own way much of the time.

Joanie, a pretty woman in her late fifties, has no major regrets. Still, she finds the little negligences bother her. "I find myself hoping," she said, "that my kids don't remember the Little League parents' meeting that I missed. I hope they don't remember the really nasty things I sometimes said when I was tired." She is heartened when her grown daughter, a teacher, tells her, 'So many kids today have bad parents. I'm glad I had good ones.'"

Not being able to provide a loving father to her children bothers Audrey, a physician. Her husband left her when her children were in elementary school, and she feels that they suffered because of her poor judgment. "I should have known my ex-husband was trouble," Audrey explains. "Everybody warned me. But I was in love, and I wouldn't listen. And my kids paid the price. If only I had chosen a better mate, they could have grown up in a more traditional household."

On the other side of the coin is Frances who, although she had a husband, doesn't believe she treated him fairly. "Looking back, I realize that I gave my kids the wrong example. They were my whole life. My husband got my leftover attention. That was wrong."

One of the most memorable examples comes from Maribeth, who confessed, "Maybe I worried about my children too much. When Nicky learned to drive, I bought a police scanner. Whenever he'd leave in the car, I whipped the scanner out of the closet, turned it on, and listened to see if there were any accidents. As soon as I heard him come home, I'd hurry and put it away so that he didn't know I'd been listening. I couldn't help it. I just had to know that he was okay. But maybe I was a little overprotective."

When Tom and Brenda Preston, Family Life Conference speakers, discuss the troublesome years in their own family, they refer to the second chapter of Joel, verse 25, where our good God says: "I will repay you for the years the locusts have eaten." Brenda knows that whatever mistakes were made can be transformed through grace. The locust image helps her to remember that God allows no evil unless a greater good will come of it.

Too much dwelling on past parenting faults is as nonproductive as it is sinful. We are accountable for our mistakes; however, the mistakes, grievous as they are, form only one thread in the fabric of motherhood. Most mothers do more things right than wrong.

REMEMBER THE GOOD

A woman in her early forties talked with me about the mistakes of motherhood. She said, "It's like that new peanut butter commercial. This mom comes on the TV and says, 'Motherhood doesn't come with a set of instructions.' That's how I feel. I learned as I went along." As mothers we take comfort from every available source—even peanut butter commercials! Reassurance can come from unexpected sources. A medieval knight brought me great comfort.

In the Cleveland Museum of Art stands an armored knight on horseback. He's been standing there for decades. My own father took me to see the knight when I was a child. In turn, I took my kids to visit this medieval fellow when they were small. My son, Joseph, called me one day during his freshman year in college. He'd just visited the art museum. "Mom," he said, "the knight's still there. Some father was explaining about armor to his son. It made me think about you and how lucky I am to have a mom who took me to the art museum."

The phone call made me weep from sheer joy. It delights me down to my bones that my son visits museums, thinks of me when he's in them, then calls home to thank me. I must have done something right.

A baby provided me with another, more vivid reminder of all the good that mothering calls forth from us. Three days before a recent Christmas I volunteered to watch the two-month-old baby of one of our friends, who was helping to deliver Christmas baskets. The baby was awake when he arrived but quickly fell asleep in his infant seat, watching the Christmas lights twinkling on the tree.

I was baking cookies in the kitchen when he woke up and started to cry. I immediately turned off the oven and gathered him up in my arms. Then we just played. I sang for him my whole repertoire of songs. We danced in front of the twinkling tree. We talked about world politics and Christmas. And God granted me the grace to remember that, with my own children, I did the very same things.

My children and I danced Christmas tree dances. We sang. Again and again, I enfolded them in my arms when they cried. Like every other mother who has ever cared for her children, I've spent invisible hours loving them—hours that no one but God will remember, but precious hours just the same.

I think of a line from *The Little Prince:* "It is the time you waste on your rose that is important." I remember Jesus admonishing Martha for not "wasting" enough time with him. The little borrowed baby reminded me that in my home there was more love than anger, more good than bad, more kindness than bitterness.

TRY NOT TO WORRY

A great-hearted woman in her nineties, who raised twelve children, once told me, "Honey, you worry too much. Just do the best you can and leave the rest to God." My father makes the same point in another way. "As a parent," he says, "you have a batting average. You do some things right and some things wrong. Even the best of parents are lucky to hit 500." Some mothers are not plagued by doubts. They take to heart the words of author Katherine Mansfield: "Regret is an appalling waste of energy; you can't build on it; it's only good for wallowing in." Laura, for example, almost dismisses out of hand the thought of regrets. "It says in Isaiah," she told me, "that we can come without paying, without cost. The Lord knows I did my best. That's all he asks."

Vera, a woman in her eighties, had a similar response to the idea of parenting mistakes: "Your generation is the only one that's ever had the time to sit around and worry about that stuff. Kids are kids. They turn out just about right no matter what we do."

There may be truth to what she says. With smaller families and modern conveniences that give us more leisure time, perhaps we have more time to brood in ways that ultimately are not helpful. A sociology professor in discussing this very topic made a rather cryptic but telling point. "Look," the professor said, "two kids will grow up with an alcoholic father. One will turn to drink and announce, 'I'm an alcoholic because my father was one.' The other kid, straight as an arrow, won't touch the stuff and he'll say, 'I'm a teetotaler because my father drank too much.'"

While we probably all agree it's better to grow up with a sober father, the professor's comments lead to another point. Whatever route we take with our children, we do not own them. They are on loan from God. Who they are and what they become is ultimately their own choice. We can shape and mold them, doing some things right and some things wrong. Ultimately, our sons and daughters belong to their Creator.

It's been a good-natured joke with my sons for years that when they grow up they can say, as did Abe Lincoln, "I owe everything I am to my sainted mother." I've always rather liked the sound of Abe Lincoln's words, even though they can't be literally true. As mothers we might like to take full credit. However, the full credit is never ours. Nor is the full blame.

THROW THE NET BACK IN

Even though we know the full blame is not ours, we cannot erase the mistakes of our past. The good news is that we are never finished with parenting. A retreat director once told a group of young mothers at a parenting conference, "God accepts us where we are as parents. You don't have to be a perfect mother and then approach God. However, God will not let you park on his time. He expects you to get moving and improve."

Always, there is room for human improvement. No parenting mistake is ever the last word. A mother I met during a routine parent-teacher conference made a lasting impression on me. When she came in to discuss her daughter's progress in my senior English class, I showed her an essay her daughter had written. In the essay, the eighteen-year-old student wrote: "I would die for my mother. Before I leave in the morning, I tell her I love her. Just in case it's the last time we see each other. She's my best friend." The mother teared up and told me: "I put that little girl through so much when she was little. I had a real drinking problem, and she really suffered. When I finally turned my life over to the Lord, things improved. And I thank Jesus every day that my daughter doesn't hold my mistakes against me. I made really bad mistakes, but I sure have tried to make up for them. I'm so glad I got a second chance."

Like the apostles in John 21 who had been unsuccessfully fishing all night, we need to pay attention to Jesus Christ. "Throw your net on the right side of the boat," he tells them, "and you will find some" (21:6). Once they did as Christ told them, the apostles had more fish than they could handle. So too, as parents, we keep throwing the net back in, knowing that, with our hearts and minds anchored in Jesus Christ, the yield will be great.

A GIFT OF GRACE

On a trip to the Holy Land I visited a church called Saint Peter in Gallicantu (Cock crow). This church overlooking the Kidron valley was built over the traditional site of the house of Caiaphas, the high priest. It is believed that in the area of this church Jesus endured his first trial, his scourging, and Peter's betrayal.

Few places in Israel grabbed ahold of me as did Saint Peter's Church. Walking on steps that Jesus used on Holy Thursday is soul-shaking enough, but the real horror and overwhelming sadness came as I stood in the dungeon, the holding cell where we believe Jesus spent the early hours of Good Friday before his crucifixion.

The place is small and cold, dreary and hard. Prisoners were lowered into its pit through a hole in the ceiling. With no source of natural light, the place is pitch dark—and horrible. My own flesh felt as if it were shrinking away from my bones as I leaned up against the cold, rockhard walls, thinking about a naked and bloodied Jesus Christ huddled in a heap on the dungeon's stone floor. Never have I been any place on earth that's made me more mindful of my sins and failings, my own betrayals. I could almost hear myself saying with Saint Peter, "I do not know the man."

Something about the earthen color of the stone brought one particular failing to my mind. The memory was such a bleak one that I tried to force it away. But the color of the stone, almost a terra-cotta, set off a series of connections in my brain, and there was no fighting off the memory. So, standing there in the dungeon, I let myself remember.

One night, when my three children were small—and the pressures were enormous, I was very lonely. It was past midnight. My husband had been due home from choir practice at ten, and I had no idea where he was.

When he finally came home at 12:30, he explained to me that a parishioner had needed to talk to him after choir practice. So they'd gone out for a cup of coffee. I was furious. Here I was alone again, while my husband had coffee with a church member at twelve o'clock at night. In my anger, I picked up a terra-cotta statue he had bought for me and smashed it against the wall. The statue was of a young mother holding a small child in her arms.

Leaning against the wall of the dungeon, I could still feel the rage of that night. I could see the ruined statue in chunks on the living room rug. I had loved the carving of the mother and child. Through the years I'd often thought of the smashed figurine with real remorse.

As I stood in the dungeon of Saint Peter's Church, I

prayed again for forgiveness of that long ago betrayal—
that night when I, like Saint Peter, acted as if I did not
know Christ.

Slowly and with a leaden heart, I walked out of the
dungeon, in search of my husband and the rest of our
group. They were in the small gift shop adjoining the
church, talking. Not wanting to interrupt their conversation, I just wandered around the gift shop, paying no
particular attention to anything, still overcome by the
experience of the dungeon.

Then out of the corner of my eye I saw her, standing
on a glass shelf in the gift shop, a terra-cotta statue of a
woman with her right hand resting gently on the head of
a small child at her side. In her left hand, she held a
water jar. I started to cry right there in the gift shop.
Walking over to take a closer look at the statue, I was
touched by the softness of her face. Had the statue spoken, the words could not have come more clearly: "Your
sins have been forgiven you. Let them go."

As I write, the statue of the woman and child sits on
my desk. She is a gift from a gracious husband and an
even more gracious God. When I look at her, she does
not remind me of the shattered statue from so many
years ago. Nor does she call forth the memory of an
overwrought and enraged young mother.

All I see is a mother and child, one of the most
blessed connections on earth.

IN GOD'S PRESENCE

Before beginning, review the prayer exercise at the end
of chapter 1.

1) Remember you are God's beloved daughter.

2) Allow yourself to remember an incident when you fell short as a mother. As you relive the memory, visualize Christ as a witness to the event. See him standing next to you, watching as you work your way through a difficult situation. Try to see your actions through the eyes of Christ.

3) Talk to Christ about what you learned when you looked at yourself through his eyes.

4) Offer a concluding prayer.

CHAPTER 6

I DON'T HAVE TO COOK DINNER TONIGHT!

My daughter, Francesca, is the neighborhood Mary Poppins, the universal nanny. She could be a full-time babysitter, if school didn't interfere. A steady stream of mothers call her, hoping that she'll be free to babysit.

As a diversionary tactic, Francesca often brings her charges to our house. It's fun having little people around. There are few things in this world that make me happier than playing with a squishy baby. Showing four-year-old boys my train layout is great fun, too. Setting an extra place at the dinner table, complete with telephone books to raise the height of the seat, is a special delight. All these children reaffirm my belief that "the kingdom of heaven belongs to such as these" (Matthew 19:14).

However . . .

All of these borrowed children remind me of the frantic pace and unending workload of child-raising years—years when we're lucky to eat a forkful of food without having to scrape mashed peas from a baby's face, years when we seldom go up and down the stairs without carrying a child or five loads of laundry.

Sometimes when a mother calls to ask my daughter to babysit, and I have to inform the woman that my daughter is unavailable, I can almost feel desperation coming through the phone. It is a desperation I remember well.

Just last night my husband and I checked in on our friend, George, to see how he fared at a horse show that morning. As we walked in, George, who was balancing his six-month-old grandson on his knee, looked up at us wearily and sighed, "Anybody is nuts to want to do this again. This kid was up every three hours last night, wanting to eat." As we all commiserated about the endless demands of raising small children, I found myself thinking of a verse from Galatians, "My dear children . . . I am again in the pains of childbirth until Christ is formed in you" (4:19). George, my husband, and I breathed a collective sigh of relief that we were past the "labor pain" part of our lives.

On Sunday mornings, when I watch other mothers struggling to keep their charges in line at church, I am happy to have my turn at that chore finished. In the grocery store, as I see moms shopping with two and three little ones in tow, I am grateful to gather my groceries alone. When I visit the doctor's office and see exhausted mothers with feverish children on their laps, my sympathy for them is mixed with gratitude that my own days of walking the floors with sick children are past.

Having these demands behind me is nice. For the first time in my adult life, there are now stretches of time when I do not have to cook, launder, chauffeur, or clean. When my husband has a late meeting and my daughter is at play practice, I have the luxury of not cooking or even thinking about what to cook. So while it may be hard to have empty places at the dinner table, there is a compensation. Sometimes we don't have to cook dinner at all!

NEWFOUND FREEDOMS

One Friday afternoon after all the students were gone, I was chatting with a colleague in my office. We both realized that we had no reason to hurry home, so she and I went out to dinner. That simple event may seem absolutely meaningless to some people, but for me it was a milestone. I did not have to cook dinner. No one needed my attention that night. Half of my family didn't live at home anymore. The other half was busy. On that Friday evening, the empty nest was a freedom, not a sadness. When the noise and strain and absolute busyness of children are gone, we can indeed revel in the newfound freedoms.

Harriet, a nurse, loves being free from having to attend school activities all the time. She remembered with a groan a fashion show she attended when her daughter was in high school. "I never spent a more miserable three hours in my entire life," Harriet said. "I had just switched to the 11:00-to-7:00 shift at work. My body hadn't adjusted yet. But I promised my daughter I'd go to the fashion show, where she was modeling prom dresses. The thing started at 8:00 and didn't end until 10:45. I was so tired from having been up the whole night before and not being able to sleep that day, that I was almost crying. I stayed for the whole thing just to watch my daughter model three different dresses. I miss my daughter, but I sure don't miss having to do things like that."

A minor, unpleasant incident last spring made me realize that I, too, am growing accustomed to the freedom. Both our boys were home on break, and my husband and I went to a concert, from which we didn't return home until 2:00 A.M. When we walked in the door, there were food-crusted dishes all over the kitchen sink. Videos were strewn all over the couch in the family room. Grubby tennis shoes littered the floor. Crumpled newspapers were scattered on the chairs. And there was a huge clump of sheet music cluttering the top of the piano.

My first reaction was one of anger. Right then my "quiver" full of children did not make me happy, as Psalm 127 suggests it will. My anger was followed by an irritation that my home had been invaded by these big lugs, who brought all this messiness with them. The next morning, when they awoke, the first thing my sons did—at my insistence—was clean up the mess. Watching them testily clean up the clutter reminded me that I'm glad to be rid of the supervisory part of parenting. With fewer people in the house, the clutter decreases exponentially, and I like not being the one to remind people to pick up after themselves.

I worked very hard to instill courtesy and respect and discipline in my children. I look at them in awe sometimes and think about what Shakespeare says of a young person in *The Winter's Tale*—they are "grown in grace and Equal with wondering." So many times, I look at my children and remember those graceful words from 1 Samuel: "I prayed for this child, and the LORD has granted me what I asked of him" (1:27). Nonetheless, I am very glad to have the hard work of raising them behind me.

We all know that motherhood is never finished, but parts of it are finite. The sheer emotional endurance required of mothers changes when the children leave. The physical demands of endless household chores lessen as suitcases are packed. No longer are the myriad details of teaching table manners, and telephone etiquette, and church behavior part of our daily activities. No longer must we play choremaster, overseeing the execution of household duties. As we cope with an empty nest, we also grow into a sense of freedom.

FEWER TENSIONS

Part of that freedom stems from a dramatic lessening of household tensions, tensions that all kinds of women speak of quite frankly. I once heard Rita Dove, the poet laureate of the United States, recall that as a child growing up in Akron she and her sisters noticed that their mother tended to disappear at odd times, especially during the summers, only to reappear without explanation. When they were grown, their mom finally explained that her disappearances were really trips to the garage. There in the garage, she sat by herself in the car, just to get some peace and quiet. Her need for peace and quiet was greater in the summer when all the kids were home from school. On first hearing this story, Rita was horrified that her mother could just walk away from her family. Once she had a daughter of her own, however, her mom's little trips to the garage became much more understandable.

Once the children are gone, we no longer have to escape to the garage to find peace. "The bathroom is so much cleaner now," my friend Mindy tells me. "I always had to fight with my daughter to put all her junk away. Now my house is peaceful and my bathroom is clean."

Suzanne, a friend of mine from graduate school, was glad to reclaim both the bathroom and the telephone. "With three teenagers in the house and only one shower, mornings and Friday nights were pretty hectic. And the telephone was always causing trouble. My husband and I set limits on shower time and phone time. It sure is nice not to have to be the 'shower police' anymore."

83

Being the "shower police" may be one of several unpleasant tasks of parenting that most of us would just as soon relinquish. God can use the reduced tension to "renew a steadfast spirit" within us (Psalm 51:10b). "I got so tired of being the enemy," Monica said, with real sadness. "I could never figure out why my daughter turned against me when she hit junior high. All of a sudden everything about me irritated her. She never really outgrew that feeling. So it's nice to not have her disapproval around all the time. I feel like so much heaviness is gone."

Shari encountered similar troubles with her teenage daughter. "One minute she loved me. The next I became Darth Vader. Somehow, it went away, though. She's in college now. I asked her the other day if she still hated me and she said, 'Oh, no, Mom. I only hated you when I was sixteen.'"

"At first," my friend Jessie said, "I thought it was just that my relationship to my husband had gotten better with the girls gone. But then I realized that I was less tense—me, all by myself. I just didn't have so much to worry about anymore. I felt, well, I guess you could say, happier, less weighted down."

"What I don't miss," Ann, a church member, told me, "is waiting up for my daughter until all hours of the night. Once she started to date, my weekends became exhausting. I hated waiting up for her, especially since my husband was snoring soundly in the bed next to me."

With an almost comic predictability, women paint this picture of a sound-asleep husband and a wide-awake mother. This model mother waits for the sound of the footsteps on the step or the jingle of keys in a pocket or the closing of the front door. And although a too quiet house can be painful, it is indeed a pleasure to be free from standing watch.

Gloria tells an embarrassing story about her own days of worrying. "Even though we live in a small town, when my daughter started dating I became a nervous wreck. Every single time the emergency siren went off and she wasn't home, I worried that her date had wrecked the car and she was in a ditch somewhere. One night, about midnight, an ambulance went by our house, with its siren on. I got this awful feeling that my daughter was in trouble. I don't know why. So I got in my car, still in my bathrobe, and followed the ambulance down the street. But, of course, the ambulance stopped at the house of an old man who'd been sick. My daughter wasn't in trouble. I only worried that she was."

Probably few of us have actually chased ambulances, but many of us know the gnawing worry that can consume us. One woman said, "Just call me Mrs. Worrywart. I can't help it." The worrying may never stop, even though Christ himself admonishes us against it, but the immediate reasons for worrying lessen when the children leave home. Perhaps as the children leave we can finally come to accept the words of Christ: "So do not worry, saying, 'What shall we eat?' or 'What shall we drink?' or 'What shall we wear?' For the pagans run after all these things, and your heavenly Father knows that you need them. But seek first his kingdom and his righteousness, and all these things will be given to you as well. Therefore do not worry about tomorrow" (Matt. 6:31-34a).

It wasn't worry that caused the greatest tension in our household. Many of our headaches came from having three very articulate children. Like many parents, we encouraged our kids to be articulate. Rightly or wrongly, I discussed presidential elections and world affairs with my older son before he was old enough to read. My kids and I talked about everything—the weather, groceries, their friends.

85

Many times, before my children reached the age of reason, I'd toss them into my little blue Volkswagen bug—Tinkerbelle, we called it—and drive across town to see my mom. As we drove along the Lake Erie shoreline, we had great conversations. Of course, half the time, my sons and daughter had no idea what we were talking about, but they knew I was paying attention to them and listening for their responses. They learned to express their opinions.

One of the traits I most cherish in my children is their ability to express themselves. It's also one of the traits that can make me want to lock myself in my room and retreat to the sixteenth century by reading one of Shakespeare's plays. The freedom of not having to listen to several different opinions about a given issue is a relief. I am relieved that my older son's running commentary on everything I do is no longer part of my existence. Watching country music videos without having to justify my musical tastes to my second son, the conservatory student, is also a nice switch.

When my son Joseph was home for Christmas, I found him standing in front of the refrigerator, with the door wide open, dawdling, while he figured out what he wanted to eat.

"Joey," I told him. "You're letting all the cold air out of the refrigerator. Figure out what you want to eat and close the door."

Appearing to ignore me, he continued to dawdle while he announced, "That's not true. We learned in physics that any temperature drop occurs in the first minute. No further damage is done if the door remains open."

Who cared about physics? This was my house, my refrigerator, and I wanted a closed refrigerator door, not a lecture on physics.

Before too long, we become accustomed to the comforts and freedoms of the empty nest. We like having less to worry about. Doing only one load of laundry instead of three is a great relief. If we stay open to its benefits, we come to see how much we can gain when our children leave home.

IMPROVED FINANCES

Along with newfound freedom and fewer domestic tensions comes another major advantage—an improved financial situation. Women were almost sheepish as they talked about the extra money they were starting to notice. As Christians we take to heart the New Testament warning: "For the love of money is a root of all kinds of evil. Some people, eager for money, have wandered from the faith and pierced themselves with many griefs" (1 Tim. 6:10). Still, like the mother of the bride who told me, "Finally, this dollar is for me," many women look forward to increased financial security.

It is rather pleasant not to have to open our wallets every single day. A whole week can pass without someone needing money for a haircut or a video or a tux or a gym uniform. Grocery bills are reduced by hundreds of dollars a month. Car insurance premiums finally start to lower as the kids move away. Our children begin to clothe themselves, and we no longer have to buy their shoes and boots and coats.

So while college may bring with it a whole new set of expenses, the daily financial drain slows—and we may go an entire month without hearing someone say: "Mom, I need lunch money."

If the daily financial demands in our own household hadn't already somewhat abated, I could not own Benvolio, my horse. When my older son left home, so I tell him, he was replaced by a four-footed, one-thousand-pound animal. This animal, a four-year-old quarterhorse, has become a good companion. The stable is one of my favorite spots, far away from my study and books and papers. Tossing hay into my horse's stall clears my mind. Cleaning my saddle is a great diversion. Riding my horse, even at my very tame speeds, keeps me active.

I never could have pursued riding when my children were small. One of the local horse breeders, a young woman in her thirties, told me, "The horses are our children. If we had kids, there'd be no time or money for the horses." I know what she means.

A friend of mine, a single mother, started skating when her children left home. She bought herself a pair of figure skates and went to an indoor rink one night a week. She liked the activity so much that she started taking lessons. Before long, her coach told her she should buy a better pair of skates. She was good enough to compete.

When this friend bought her first skating outfit, she called me with absolute glee in her voice. "You should see this thing," she said, her voice bounding through the phone. "It's blue and chiffonny and it's got sequins!"

Sequins! The last thing on earth this woman ever had money for when she was raising her children was sequins. Now, she glides along the ice, freed by the empty nest.

Peggy, another friend, quit her second job as a waitress to work in a shelter for battered women and children. Now that her own brood is gone, she finds that the second job is unnecessary; and she likes helping other women who are struggling to keep their families together. "I was never interested in doing volunteer work when the kids were home. I was too busy working two jobs," Peggy says.

Like Peggy, many other women discover that an

improved financial situation provides new opportunities for giving to God.

Our God is one of endless possibilities, who offers us many chances to enjoy the world and our lives.

WE ARE PLEASING TO GOD

There are, then, pronounced advantages to an empty nest. I've come to suspect that, as women, we are a bit reluctant to throw up our hands and shout, "Thank goodness my kids are gone!" But, there is no suppressing the gleam in my friend Lori's eye when she says, "At last I can have my own sewing room." Or the giggle in Mitsy's tone when she says, "Finally, I get the whole chicken breast for myself."

I have come to a realization. As Christians, we are very accustomed to believing that unless we are doing something for someone else, we are not fulfilling Christ's mandate. However, God's is the glory whether we bake bread, change diapers, or go whitewater rafting. We are no less pleasing to God if we read a book instead of scrubbing a floor.

Our Christianity is framed by the notion of sacrificing ourselves so that others might live. Mothers do that in the most literal sense when they allow their bodies to be taken over by another person. But the freedom of the empty nest allows us to define ourselves in new ways. Always with our eye on the Lord, we see that shedding the skin of full-time mothering can bring forth a new person tucked inside, waiting to step into another kind of sunlight.

As a young mother I attended a women's church meeting. The speaker talked about how to make mundane household chores seem more uplifting. "Don't just think that you're waxing a floor," the speaker said. "Remember that you're waxing it so that someone you love can walk on it. Don't complain about folding laundry. Thank God that someone you love will wear the laundry that you fold. Every task you do can be transformed, if you only remember that you are doing it for someone else. Only those things you do for others are worthy in the sight of God."

Even then, her comments grated against my sensibilities. I knew what she was trying to say—that only those things we do for other people are worthwhile. However, our purpose on earth is to know, love, and serve God. Sometimes we fulfill that purpose by serving others. Sometimes we fulfill those tasks by watching a sunset and eating a hot fudge sundae. God does not erase us from the slate of life because we do not serve other people every moment. We can glorify, praise, and adore God in every facet of our existence. God must be smiling as my friend glides along the ice in chiffon and sequins.

Christ spent so much time in the wilderness, alone. He was not praying every single minute. No one can. Still, we would never suggest that Christ's time in the Judean wilderness was wasted. His time away from other people helped make him who he was. As people who carry the name of Christ, we will never abandon our efforts to advance his kingdom on earth. We will do all the good we can for as long as we can. In doing good, we will always be aware of others' needs. But our own lives, even when we are not actually serving the needs of others, are precious in God's sight.

IN GOD'S PRESENCE

1) Read the following Scripture passages:
   Matthew 4:1
   Matthew 14:13*a*
   Luke 22:39-41

2) In each of these passages, Jesus withdrew to be alone with God in prayer. Think about the places you like to go to be alone with God.

3) Now read these Scripture passages:
Luke 5:27-32
Luke 7:36
Luke 10:38-39

4) In each of these passages, Jesus was invited to a dinner party. Think about the times and places you enjoy the company of others.

5) Offer a concluding prayer in which you thank God for giving us stories of a Savior who was pleasing to God in all situations—whether he was alone in the wilderness or among many people at a dinner party. Even when he was socializing, Jesus was doing God's work.

CHAPTER 7

WHERE DO I GO FROM HERE?

Commenting on her role as a mother, Jacqueline Kennedy Onassis said, "I consider it the most important thing I've ever done in my life. The thing I care most about is the happiness of my children. If you fail in that, nothing could ever matter very much." The matriarch of the Kennedy family, Rose, said of motherhood, "I have always looked on child rearing not only as a work of love and duty, but as a profession that was fully as interesting and challenging as any honorable profession in the world, and one that demanded the best I could bring to it."

These strong feelings about the central importance of raising children are shared by most mothers. We know that God has given us few tasks more important than the care and nurture of our sons and daughters. A neighbor of mine told me, "All I ever wanted to be was a mother. If I died right now, I'd be okay because I've done what God wanted me to do in raising my kids."

It has been said, "Our children are our messengers to the future." We can rejoice in a job well done when we look at those messengers and realize that they are shining witnesses to God's glory. Once our "messengers" have left home, however, we face the challenge of redirecting our energies and talents. Although our children will continue to need us and occasionally demand our time and energy, the empty nest presents us with abundant opportunities to pursue new paths, follow new adventures, and work in larger capacities for the kingdom of God.

No matter what choices we've made when our children were growing up, their leaving home presents us with new decisions. Whether we've been full-time homemakers or mothers who worked outside of the home, the empty nest gives us more time. We best not squander that time—there is much work to be done.

After we get reacquainted with our spouse, after we get used to the fact that we don't have to cook dinner every night, we face yet another transition: Where do we go from here? Given our talents and abilities, how can we best serve in the world?

Few of us will ever list *mothering* on our résumés, but every one of us knows that mothering helped us to become the women we are. Everything from our organizational skills to our compassion has been tried and tested as we've juggled the demands of our growing families. We've learned to put our own needs on the back burner; however, we've also learned that we need to take care of ourselves. As we survey the years ahead of us, we know that we are equipped for a variety of pursuits. Discerning God's will for us once our children are grown is a vital task.

Lori, a woman in her early fifties who resumed her teaching career after her children were grown, spoke of a time when she was offered a full-time teaching job when her children were small. After she accepted the position, she realized that she'd made a mistake, so she called the school principal and withdrew her acceptance. "I just knew, all those years ago, that my place was in the home. But now that my kids have left, I've gone back to full-time teaching, and I love it. I never regretted staying home. But I'm so glad God has given me another shot at the classroom."

June, who returned to her career as a dietitian once her last child left, explains: "I always kind of did something when the kids were small. I mean I never was idle. I did some substitute teaching. I edited the Kiwanis newsletter. I did volunteer work. But I never wanted to make a full-time commitment outside of the home. Now, it's great though. I love my job. I feel so lucky."

A registered nurse, Gayle never put aside her nursing. She relied on flexible shifts to help her juggle career and family, even as she raised her family. Now that her children are gone she is pursuing new medical opportunities. "When a new pediatrician came to town," Gayle explains, "she asked me if I'd be interested in working with her as a nurse practitioner. My husband and I talked about it and decided that I should take the job. It's been great. With my kids gone, I have so much more time to spend with patients."

PRAY ALWAYS

God tells us in Isaiah 49:6, "I will give you as a light to the nations, that my salvation may reach to the end of the earth" (NRSV). The verse expresses God's great hope in us, and it gives us an important responsibility. We are to be the light of the nations.

Becoming the light of the nations is a lifelong task, one that will never be finished. The empty nest encourages us to reevaluate our own lights. Prayer is a vital part of this reevaluation. We cannot know God's plan for us; we cannot answer the question, "Where do I go from here?" unless we train ourselves to hear our creator's voice. We won't recognize God's voice in the whisper, if all we pay attention to are the trumpets.

Mattie, one of the holiest women I've ever known, was once asked in a Sunday school class to explain how she prayed. This eighty-year-old woman with sparkling blue eyes and white hair did not hesitate. "Why, I just sit still and let God love me." Her answer so intrigued me that when I drove her home after church, I asked her to explain what she meant. As we pulled into her driveway, Mattie turned to me and said, "Well, come here, I'll show you."

I followed her into her home, a small bungalow. She headed for what looked like a closet, but when she opened the door, I was stunned. "This is my prayer room," she said. In the very small room was a chair, a reading lamp, a small table on which there was an open Bible. A lush Swedish ivy plant hung from a planter in the window.

In my previous, frequent visits to Mattie's home, she never mentioned the room, and I'd never seen it. Seeing the surprised look on my face, she said: "This room is the most special place in the house. It is where I wait on the Lord." This human being radiated the love of God, a love that grew as she prayed. I wanted to follow her example.

Within a month, I had carved out a space for a prayer room in our home. And we've had one ever since. In our current home, the room is a very small space in the back of the house. When we first moved in the room was a closet, filled with old rolls of wallpaper, bookshelves, and broken shutters. My husband and I cleared away the debris, painted the walls and bought a rug for the floor. We added a chair, a plant, a reading lamp, and a small table.

The only thing that happens in the room is prayer. No

one eats in the room or watches TV. No one has ever argued in the room or been ill in the room. The space is reserved for prayer. There is a particular power that emanates from such a space. Mattie had told me, "I think of prayer rooms as so many little lighted candles, waiting for the return of the Bridegroom. Just think if every Christian household had a space reserved solely for prayer. When the Lord returns, how pleased he will be."

Of course, it is true that we can pray anywhere, anytime. We don't need to lock ourselves in a closet. However, it is also true that Jesus Christ frequently went off by himself to pray. And his isolated prayer helped him to discern his father's will. Because the empty nest is such a major life transition, we need to be acutely alert to God's presence in our lives. By nudging us to stay in daily communication with God, a prayer room might offer us new ways to hear divine whispers.

Only through prayer do we come to know what God wants of us. If we know who we are as we stand before God, almost everything else in life falls into place. Most women have many names. Their husbands call them by one name, their friends by another, their parents by another. When God speaks to you, by what name are you called?

Immersing ourselves in the Gospels draws us closer to God. Reading passages in the Old Testament gives us a clear sense of God's working through history. Sitting still and letting God love us can be one of the best forms of prayer. Certainly, we will want to ask God to meet the needs of our family and friends. We will want to thank God for all our blessings. We will want to offer praise. Yet in all our prayer, we have to create a space to hear God's voice, so that we know what is being asked of us.

"If I didn't pray all the time, how would I ever have known God wanted me to work in the church?" Suzanne asked. "For about five years after my children left, I volunteered in a nursing home, and I kept praying, asking God what I should really be doing with my life. Then one night when I was praying, it hit me. I had always wanted a career in church work. So I went to seminary and, at 57, I graduated with my degree in Christian education. Now I work full-time for the Lord. And I've never stopped praying."

Just about the time I began to realize that my own children were really going to be leaving home, I had a very tough decision to make. As I grew into the realization that my years of raising children were about over, I was offered a teaching position at the United States Naval Academy.

The day of my campus interview I was pretty confused. The prospective job was a superb one, with warm-hearted colleagues, bright students, a beautiful campus. The hectic pace of my interview did nothing to clear up my confused head. Before I even visited Annapolis, I had begged God, pleaded with God to let me know what I was supposed to do. Was this the job that God wanted me to take as my nest emptied?

Wandering around the campus, I tried, futilely, to pray. As I examined historical cannons and memorial torpedoes and old anchors, I wondered what on earth God could want me to do at such a place. Others were far more suited to the military atmosphere. By the time I found my way into the Academy chapel, I had convinced myself of two things: (1) God and the Navy had nothing in common, and (2) I'd better refuse the job if it were offered.

In this preoccupied and self-centered state, I ambled down the left aisle of the chapel on my way to the front altar. The first stained-glass window stopped me. On it was etched this passage from Mark: "And he began to teach them by the seaside; and there was gathered unto him a great multitude so that he entered into a ship" (4:1). Before that moment, it never occurred to me that the gospel had a nautical theme. The second window bore this inscription: "What manner of man is this that even the winds and the sea obey him?" (Matt. 8:27). "Come ye after me and I will make you to become fishers of men" was engraved on the third window (Mark 1:17). And finally, the fourth window: "Fear not, Paul: God hath given thee all them that sail with thee"(Acts 27:24). By the time I reached the front of the chapel, I felt as if I'd just received a lesson in the nautical gospel, a lesson that forced me to confront my own spiritual blindness.

Now eager for more nautical lessons, I zipped across the front of the chapel, heading for the next set of windows. But a large, sky-blue window above a door made me stop moving. Here was a window without a gospel message. It did not need one.

The picture formed in stained glass was perfectly clear. Against a sky-blue background, near an American flag, stood a young naval officer in his dress whites. He held his hat in his right hand, as he read his commission. In the background, with his right hand extended in a blessing, was Jesus Christ. As I stood staring up at the window, the sun pierced through its blue, stained glass.

Right then, I understood in a new way the omnipresence of the Creator. If I'd been unable to find the Lord of Life in this turn of events, if I truly believed that God wasn't in the Navy, that was nobody's fault but my own.

The sons and daughters of women just like me would come to the Naval Academy. It could be said,

"Fear not: God hath given thee all them that sail with thee."

I was not accustomed to hearing God's voice on windows, and I certainly had never had a conversation with God about the Navy. All my efforts to force God's hand had been fruitless. God's hand cannot be forced. But if we stay open to all possibilities, God's will can be made manifest.

WHAT IS OUR MISSION?

Continual prayer, then, will help us to discern God's will. Each of us has a mission in life that is never finished. A preacher in a tent revival told his audience that there was an easy way to figure out if we'd done all that God wanted us to do on this earth. "It's real simple," the preacher said. "If you're still alive, you're not done."

As long as we live, there is good to be accomplished. As long as we wake up on this side of heaven, there are people who need us and tasks to be undertaken. Grounded firmly in prayer we can make the choices about what our future will look like.

There is always a danger of being overly busy. We may be tempted, at first, to take on too many new assignments at work, to volunteer for one too many days at the nursing home, to sign up for one too many church committees. But, in one lifetime we cannot accomplish all the things that we can imagine. And that's good news. We want our dreams to outnumber our years.

Our churches always need our talents. Nursing homes always need additional volunteers. Hospitals often need volunteers to deliver flowers and cards, to deliver patients to their rooms. Reading for persons who are visually impaired offers another opportunity to do good work. Once we put on the mind and heart of Christ, our problem becomes choosing among all the possibilities. There are opportunities all around us.

There was a woman in our neighborhood whom my children referred to as "The Blueberry Muffin Lady." I never even saw this woman, but she somehow discovered that my sons liked blueberry muffins. Whenever she made a batch, she'd phone me and say, "Send one of the boys down. I've made some muffins." When she died, I learned that she'd been performing similar acts of generosity for generations. She was a shut-in, really, and couldn't get out of the house much. But she could make people happy by baking for them.

Lucy had a similar quiet ministry. Confined to a wheelchair as a result of an automobile accident, Lucy developed a prayer ministry. "My accident happened right after all my children were gone. I almost died, but everybody's prayers pulled me through. Once I got better, I asked God to show me what I could do from a wheelchair. Well, he sure showed me."

Lucy's family and friends, knowing she was a woman of prayer, started giving her the names of people who needed her prayers. At first Lucy was praying for only a few people. Then, as word spread, Lucy was swamped with prayer requests. "I guess it made people feel good to know that I had so much time to pray for them," Lucy suggests. Now she has developed an active ministry. She's enlisted the help of several of her friends, and among them, they respond to every prayer request that comes their way.

Mary Ellen, after her children left home, threw herself into a flurry of God-given activity. And she has the energy to sustain her whirlwind pace. If a shut-in needs a prescription, Mary Ellen runs to the drugstore. If a young mother needs a babysitter in a pinch, Mary Ellen is there. If one of her grown children needs help moving, Mary Ellen is there with the U-Haul. "I thought about going back to work," Mary Ellen says, "but I've got too much to do. I don't want to be tied down to some job." God has given her the talents and the resources to respond to a variety of needs. She has great energy, financial security, and an enormous heart.

Then there's Justine, a school librarian, who wouldn't know what to do if she stayed home. "Sure, juggling everything has been hard at times, but God has always made it very clear to me, my career is part of my ministry. My two daughters were so proud to come to work with me when they were little. Even now, when they're home on break, they come to the school and help me catalog new books. Or they read to the kindergarten classes. They love the library as much as I do. My career has been an important part of what we've been as a family."

It was Fiona, a pastor's wife in England, who said most clearly what so many women have experienced firsthand. One day after I visited a city mission that she and her husband started in their London church, this gentle-souled woman served me tea and scones. Knowing I was also a pastor's wife, she said "Well, between your husband's church and your family, you must be very busy." For a split second, I thought about letting her assumption stand. For some reason, I didn't want to tell her that, in addition to being a pastor's wife and mother of three, I had pursued my own career. But, of course, I did tell her the truth. What she said has stayed with me. "I think the good Lord lets us know what He wants us to do. I've always felt that He wanted me to work side by side with my husband in the church. That way I could tend his flock and my own at the same time. But if God had let me know that he wanted me to be doing something else, I wouldn't have said 'No.' You can't say 'No' to God. Not when you know in your heart that he has things for you to do."

THIS IS GOD'S WORK

God works differently in all of our lives. There are Marys and there are Marthas. In discerning God's will some women stay home. Others decide that God calls them to assume multiple roles. Only we can decide what path to pursue. It may be that others will criticize our choices, but we are heartened by the voice of Jesus. "Why do you trouble the woman? She has performed a good service for me" (Matt. 26:10b NRSV). Saint Augustine said it another way, "Love and do what you will."

In Exodus, we read, "He has filled them with skill to do all kinds of work" (35:35). The desire to work, to do something for the Lord, no matter if it's in the home or outside of it, is part of our God-given nature. The multiplicity of tasks that we undertake can also be God-given. When the disciples asked Jesus "What must we do to do the works God requires?" Jesus answered, "The work of God is this: to believe in the one he has sent" (John 6:28-29). Women of faith who keep their hearts and minds set on Jesus Christ can learn what he is calling them to do.

God set Adam and Eve to work in the Garden of Eden before the Fall. Like Adam and Eve, we are the tenders of God's garden, the earth. We will be forever at work improving and adorning that which God has created. Throughout our lives we will have choices about which parts of that garden to tend. Our labors take on one character in our child-raising years, and our efforts take on added dimensions as we are freed from those early responsibilities.

In his post-Resurrection appearance to Peter, which is recorded in the twenty-first chapter of John's Gospel, Jesus repeatedly asks Peter "Do you love me?" When Peter responds affirmatively, Jesus gives him these commands: "Feed my lambs"; "Take care of my sheep"; "Feed my sheep." If Peter loves Jesus then he will work for the Lord's kingdom, and he will do it now. Jesus does not use the past tense in his commands. He uses the present tense. *Feed. Take care. Feed.* Work for me now. What you did yesterday is over; what you might do tomorrow has not yet come to pass. Take care of my people today.

Our years of rocking the cradle are in the past. In the years when ours is the hand that rocks the cradle, most of us are aware that we do "rule the world." For me, no professional accomplishment ever matches the sheer joy and pride I feel as I look at my grown children. Sitting in a church or a concert hall, for example, listening to my son play his trumpet makes me exuberantly happy. I have a son who makes music. That fact matters to me more than any of my temporal accomplishments. I thank God for giving me the chance to raise three human beings. One of the most important tasks God gives us is the raising of our children. But when our children are grown and finding their own way through life, we have even more work to do for the Lord.

The ability and the desire to do God's work are gifts. We are lucky indeed if the choices we make relative to those gifts can also be God-given. Truly we are blessed if the Lord stirs us up so that we can begin "to work on the house of the LORD" (Haggai 1:14), because when we are stirred, we know that God's house can never, never be empty.

IN GOD'S PRESENCE

1) Call to mind the variety of roles you assume on a daily basis: mother, wife, sister, friend, employee, choir member, gardener, etc. (You might even want to create a written list.)

2) Write down all the different names by which you are called. Do you know by what names God addresses you? By what name were you called during the prayer exercises at the end of chapter 1?

3) Read John 21:15-17.

4) Ask Christ to help you discern how you can presently advance his kingdom.

CHAPTER 8

THE NEST IS NOT REALLY EMPTY

After a busy Saturday, I flopped down on my bed, ready to sleep. I decided to thank God for all the blessings of the day. My thank-you list included: a great morning ride on my horse; a long overdue lunch with an old friend; phone calls from both of my sisters; the chance to see a new movie; a glorious thirty-minute nap; and an abiding sense of God's presence during the day.

Only as I started to drift off to sleep did the realization dawn on me. My husband and children played no part in this day. The boys were at college. My husband and daughter were away on a weekend retreat. I hadn't done much of anything for anyone that day. But God's presence had been very real.

So as I fell asleep, I added one more thing to my thank-you list: a growing understanding that the nest is not really empty.

In Matthew 17, there is an incident that draws attention to a true understanding of emptiness. The temple tax collectors are harassing Peter, and they ask him: "Does your teacher not pay the temple tax?" Jesus, in an attempt to soothe a potentially testy situation, tells Peter: "Go to the sea and cast a hook; take the first fish that comes up, and when you open its mouth, you will find a coin; take that and give it to them for you and me" (24, 27 NRSV).

This particular type of fish, which is now called "St. Peter's Fish," carries its fertilized eggs in its mouth. Once the baby fishes hatch, they swim out of the fish's mouth to start life on their own. But the mother fish, in an attempt to fill the empty space, stores other objects in her mouth—coins, small rocks, bottle caps, bits of broken plastic. Routinely, odd bits and pieces are found in the mouths of these fishes. The coin Peter finds in the fish's mouth in Matthew 17 is a replacement for a missing baby.

We are saved from the need to fill up our empty nests with "stuff" by our faithful understanding that God is with us; consequently, no place in the universe is empty. Saint-Exupéry aptly captures an eternal truth in his book, *The Little Prince:* "It is only with the heart that one can see rightly." Our eyes and ears may perceive a vacuum; however, our hearts understand the deeper truth. With our solitary hearts yoked to the heart of Jesus Christ, we can transform all the seemingly empty spaces of the universe into places of shining love. The freedom we gain when our children walk away from us increases our ability to discover who we are as we stand before God. The greatest personal strength of character and conviction flows from an unshakable understanding of who Jesus Christ says that we are, of knowing that name by which he addresses us.

In the midst of children moving out and anxieties setting in; in the midst of whirlwind upheavals and flurried leave-takings; in the midst of our very real tears and our very deep losses, we hear the only voice that matters: "Be still, and know that I am God" (Ps. 46:10a).

As part of a biblical seminar my husband and I took during our trip to Israel, we had the option of taking a three-hour trek through the Judean wilderness. In explaining the trip, the instructor warned us that the hike was treacherous. Just the previous week, a monk, who was very familiar with the terrain, had fallen to his death. Sometimes, the professor warned us, people had heart attacks on the trip. "However," he added, "most people, hundreds of people, survive the hike without incident."

The Judean wilderness is breathtakingly beautiful; and it is the desert where Jesus was tempted by the devil and where he often retreated to pray. My desire to be in the midst of such a place overcame my common sense, and I decided to go on the journey.

Physical coordination has never been one of my talents, but I hoped that my simple desire to make the trek through the desert would outweigh my natural clumsiness. I was absolutely, horribly wrong.

Within twenty minutes of starting out on the journey, I understood both the treachery of the trail and the stupidity of my own decision. Somebody like me, who's been hospitalized with vertigo attacks, was insane to be walking on a rocky path less than a yard wide, a path that dropped off suddenly and mercilessly into a rocky canyon. The path was not guarded by any rail or natural growth.

The trip was going to be three hours long—complete with pauses, terrifying pauses along the way when the instructor gave little lectures on points of biblical interest. There would be no turning around. I did not know how I would survive. I did the only thing I knew to do.

I prayed.

At first, it was the most mundane of prayers: "Please, God, don't let me fall off this cliff." Then, as the time passed, the prayer wasn't even a verbal one. I just pretended, as if my life depended on it, that Jesus Christ was walking next to me. For three unrelenting, dreadful hours, I made my way along this path, sometimes having to crawl on all fours in order to keep from falling. While others spotted mountain goats or gazed up at eagles, I kept my eyes fixed on the path and my mind set on God.

When the trip was done and our bus driver picked us up to bring us back to the hotel, everyone, including me, had a few good chuckles at my expense. I guess I looked pretty silly climbing over the rocks. Not until my head hit my pillow that night did the sheer terror break out of me. Finally, alone, I let myself relive the fear of those three hours and I sobbed myself to sleep.

Looking back now, I gain the oddest perspective. As I try to see myself walking along the path, I cannot imaginatively put myself back inside my trembling legs and arms. I cannot feel the rocks under my feet. Almost as if I'm in a helicopter looking down on myself walking along the path, I see myself being watched. And I look very small. This small little person is being watched with infinite care and tenderness. That day I was terrified. I had to remind myself to breathe. I had to remind my legs to move. But the recurring sense of that trip through the Judean wilderness is one of being in God's presence. There was nothing left on that journey but God. My husband was among the group, but he could not walk the path for me. My children were thousands of miles away. Nothing I had ever done in life—no meals cooked, no articles written, no degress obtained—could help me. All of those temporal things were burned away.

Just me. Just God. A crystal clear reminder that God is with us always, and that all the challenges we face in life—whether they are rocky precipices or empty nests—are faced in the presence of an indwelling God, who is closer to us than our next breath.

A NATURAL PART OF LIFE

Having read her diary and seen the play based on her life, I felt prepared for my visit to Anne Frank's secret hiding place in Amsterdam. Yet, not until I stood in Anne Frank's bedroom did the full force of her tragic story hit me. In preparation for my trip to Amsterdam, I had reread *The Diary of Anne Frank.* The book, which records the thoughts and feelings of a young Jewish girl whose family is forced into hiding by Hitler, captures some very remarkable and some very routine family tensions. Tensions between the adolescent Anne and her mother pop up all over the diary. "Just had a big bust-up with Mummy for the umpteenth time," Anne writes in her diary. "We simply don't get on these days. . . . I can understand my friends better than my own mother."

When I found myself in the Franks' hiding place, I thought of the edgy existence the poor family endured in its secret quarters. The places Anne describes in her diary are still there: the small kitchen, the tiny bathroom, Anne's shared bedroom—with her collection of movie star photos still glued to the wall.

Seeing Anne's actual diary, preserved in a glass case, is heartrending. There in its cloth, red plaid binding is the book the Nazis left behind when they raided the hiding place and forced the Frank family into concentration camps. In her graceful handwriting is Anne's story.

Anne did not live long enough to tell her mother, "Oh, I only hated you when I was sixteen." Anne's mother didn't live long enough to hear one of her grown children say, "So many kids today have bad parents. I'm glad I had good ones." There was no empty nest in the Frank household. A horrible, unnatural force ripped away the natural rhythms of the family. Somehow the dreadful visit to the Frank house made me face the empty nest with a clearer vision.

On returning to the States, I learned of the tragic death of an 18-year-old boy, killed in a freak car accident. A recent high school graduate, the boy was an honor student with a full college scholarship. The bright, lovable boy was prematurely ripped away from his parents.

The 18-year-old's death, combined with my visit to the Frank home, served as a very pointed reminder that there is nothing tragic about the emptying of our nest. Grown children leaving home is a natural and good part of life. We may be stunned, as was my older son, with "how fast this all moves forward without permission"; yet we cannot stop the movement forward. Nor do we really want to. We look the empty nest right in the eye, recognize that we must let go of certain things, then, in great faith, we move forward to glorify God. The process, clearly, is not simple. We may be tempted to blink back tears as we look into our empty nests, but when the blinking is done, there stands our God and the rest of our lives. Those things that we must abandon—the physical presence of our children, their emotional dependence on us, our own youth, our own lives—all can be turned over to Jesus Christ, the ultimate caretaker.

LETTING GO OF OUR CHILDREN'S PHYSICAL PRESENCE

The very molecules in a house can seem empty when children leave. The spaces that used to be filled with their opinions and jokes and complaints and conversation are vacated. On very quiet evenings, every vacant bed, every cleaned-out dresser drawer, every unoccupied chair emits an almost palpable sense of loss. There is no escaping, at such times, the very clear fact that our children are gone. We're not going to be bumping into them in the hallway at night, or at the breakfast table in the morning. They now inhabit other spaces.

Here again, we can be sideswiped by unexpected reminders. Bridget, a former colleague of mine, remembers the first time she watched a band parade after her son, the drum major, graduated. Bridget says, "It was a gorgeous Labor Day, and I sat out on my porch like always to watch the town parade come by. I wasn't even thinking about my son. But then, before I even saw it, I heard the high school band. And I knew I was in trouble. By the time the Band of Gold stepped into view, I was crying. There were all those kids, but my son wasn't leading them anymore. Right then, I just wanted him back. Physically. Marching in that parade like he always did."

My son's physical distance was reinforced for me in a very rudimentary way. The day we deposited Joseph at college, we agreed to meet back at his dorm room after our separate orientation meetings. Because the parent meeting ended thirty minutes before the student one, we returned to the dorm well ahead of Joey. Because the student rooms were locked, several parents milled around the adjoining common room. As I stood in front of my son's room, a silly little piece of construction paper saddened me. The dorm counselor had written each student's name on construction paper and taped the names to individual room doors. I was reminded of Joseph's kindergarten classroom, when his teacher labeled each child's desk as a sign of

113

welcome. When he started kindergarten, I led him to his desk, gave him a hug, and told him I'd pick him up in a few hours. Now, his name was on a door that I could not enter. This room was locked to me.

Several moms seemed similarly reflective. We all made efforts to be cheery when our kids were around, but in the lulls, our true feelings emerged. One mother complained about the size of the rooms: "How do they expect three kids to sleep in a room the size of a closet?" Another was furious at the unfinished bathroom: "What do they expect these kids to do? The johns aren't even finished yet." Still another lamented the inadequate desks: "My son is used to having a desk all to himself."

Our sense of loss manifested itself in these physical comments. The physical spaces that our children occupied would no longer be under our control. From the time of their conception, children evoke maternal awareness of their physical presence. We take great care to preserve all the environments our children inhabit. Once they leave home, we have to accept the fact that they will inhabit places separate from us. But the distance that separates us is not larger than the God who enfolds our children. As we stay close to God, our children stay close to us. While we pray for them, we carry them in our hearts and minds. We set them free to step into their own lives.

LETTING GO OF OUR CHILDREN'S EMOTIONAL DEPENDENCE

A "Family Circus" cartoon portrayed the very irritated cartoon mother yelling at her four children as they bounced all over the sofa, knocking over lamps. With her hands on her hips, she yells, "I wish you'd

114

GROW UP! All of you." The next frame shows a very pensive, solitary mother with her thoughts illustrated in one of those cartoon bubbles. In the bubble are her four children, fully grown, heading off to college. The last frame pictures a smiling mom, on the sofa, with her four little children gathered all around her. As she cuddles them, she says out loud, "But not too soon."

But the time comes, without our permission, when our children do move away from us. They are no longer dependent on us for their primary emotional support. We are replaced.

When my older son was ten, I made him a pillow for Christmas. I sewed his name onto the pillow, and he kept it on his bed thereafter. The stuffed twelve-inch square, with a red heart at the center, survived all of our moves. In every new place, it was a familiar bit of old places. On the day my son left for college, we were loading our family van with his belongings, when I sent my daughter back inside the house to make sure Tony hadn't forgotten anything. A few minutes later she came out with the pillow.

"Tony forgot this," she said, tossing the pillow at me.

But, of course, the pillow had not been forgotten. It had been very intentionally left behind. Leaving the kids to finish packing the van, I walked back into my son's bedroom and returned the pillow to the top bunk. There the pillow remains. Tony sees it when he comes home to visit.

No little homemade gift will provide emotional security for my son anymore. His primary emotional needs will be met elsewhere, by other people, in other places. It won't be me who sees the first signs of illness or hears his lighthearted laughter. When school wears him down, I won't be able to alleviate the pressure. Part of this process of letting go starts as soon as our children are old enough to crawl away from us. For only the shortest time, we are their sole emotional support. For a while longer, we are their primary emotional support. Subsequently, their friends and teachers and counselors step into the spaces left empty as they pull away from us.

The emotional bond linking mothers and children never ends. Nevertheless, we have to let go of our role as their primary support system. We move aside to make room for other people who come to play central roles in the lives of our children. Moving aside can be tough, but when we do we often discover a deeper awareness of God's abiding presence.

LETTING GO OF OUR YOUTH

In reading articles about the empty nest, I always dismissed the notion that part of the pain came from having to face the loss of our own youth. Being young never made much difference to me one way or the other. My kids leaving home was a totally different issue than that of my lost youth. Two minor incidents forced a deeper truth on me.

Last year I bought a baby outfit for a friend of ours who just had her second son. In her thank-you note she wrote, "Just think, in a year or two you'll have two of our little boys raiding your refrigerator and jumping on your couch. We're going to get you ready for grandchildren, you see." That last reference to grandchildren felt like a slap. What could she mean? Grandchildren? People my age were still having children of their own. Why were we being relegated to the status of grandparents? I couldn't quite articulate why her line bothered me, but it surely did.

116

Then, at a family reunion, we saw people we had not seen for almost twenty years. As they met our grown children, they laughingly told them, "Oh, we could never keep up with your parents. They kept having babies one right after the other." Person after person made reference to those early years of our marriage when we had three kids in less than four years.

Finally, I understood the barb of the thank-you note. Never again would I be the young mother with three little ones in tow. That task and that glory had now passed on to other women. No one would ever again say to me, "You're pregnant *again?*" The next decade of my life may see me step into the role of grandmother. A good part of me resists that notion. *Grandmother* sounds old. It signals someone in the second half of life.

A friend of mine came to this same realization—that we are indeed in the second half of life. One day she was listening to the radio and she heard "The Wedding Song" by Paul Stookey, of Peter, Paul and Mary. You remember the lyrics, don't you? "Well a man shall leave his mother and a woman leave her home. They shall travel on to where the two shall be as one." Popular in the sixties and seventies, the song was sung in many of our weddings. After hearing this song, my friend, Germaine, called me, very upset. "The song made me think about *my* son. The song always used to make me think about how I left home to get married. But today, all of a sudden I realized I was now the mother being left."

Somehow, through the silent stretch of the years, we have grown older. We are not the young brides to be, giggling over brides magazines and choosing china patterns. We are not the newlyweds, embarking on a brand new journey. We are not the young mothers with babies tugging on our hair. When the voices of other mothers float on the summer air, calling children home for dinner, we have no children to summon home. Our time for all of those activities is past. We keenly feel the passing away of what was once ours. But the passing away makes room for another kind of growth.

Betty Freidan in her book *The Fountain of Age* dispels many of the myths associated with the second half of life. In examining her own life as mother and grandmother, she comes to accept and revel in the freedom of maturity. In discussing her insights, Friedan says: "I am myself at this age. It took me all these years to put the missing pieces together, to confront my own age in terms of integrity and generativity, moving into the unknown future with a comfort now, instead of being stuck in the past. I have never felt so free."

Maturity does bring with it many freedoms. Most of us are calmer, wiser, more compassionate now than we were twenty years ago. Mothering has taught us flexibility and patience. We have learned that the long view is often much more important than the short one. As we acknowledge that our characters have improved with age, we become increasingly aware that it is our cooperation with the Holy Spirit that has allowed the transformation to take place. The God that helped us to outgrow the self-centeredness of youth remains with us as we continue to be transformed by grace. Always, God calls us to be better than we already are, to grow beyond what we already know. That God is with us as our children start out on their new journeys and as we start out on ours.

LETTING GO OF OUR LIVES

Jesus Christ tells us, "He who wants to gain his life must lose it." We have to accept our physical limitations, most specifically the limitation of mortality. We will die. We will not be around forever. Our children will, we hope, long outlive us. We will face death alone. No matter how many people surround us at the moment of our death, the journey is ours alone to make. There is no escape route.

I think again of my mother-in-law, who in many ways had the luckiest of deaths. Although she was in terrible pain and discomfort, she died surrounded by people who loved her. As she lived out her final days on earth, she was not abandoned in some nursing home. She spent her last days in the home where she had raised her three children. Her sons came from both coasts to be with her. Her daughter rearranged her own life in order to help her mother die in peace.

Still, at the moment when Ruth abandoned life, she abandoned it alone. No one could do that for her. Her children, no matter how devoted, could not die for her.

When the empty nest pulls, maybe even yanks, so much away from us, we are reminded that our own lives are not our own. We are God's. The flurry of activity that surrounds us in the years of raising children might temporarily mask the finite nature of our time on earth, but raising a family is not our ultimate goal. Returning to God is.

And that goal sustains us in hope. We are free to celebrate all of life's transitions because we know they are leading us to God.

119

ACTING "AS IF"

Our losses allow us to become more Christlike. Doing so requires discipline, determination, and our willingness to make room for the grace of God. At every step of our journey, we have to pitch into the trash those traits and flaws which keep us from imitating Christ. "If your right eye causes you to sin, gouge it out and throw it away. . . . If your right hand causes you to sin, cut it off and throw it away. It is better for you to lose one part of your body than for your whole body to go into hell" (Matt. 5:29-30). If your temper is your problem, throw it in the dumpster. If laziness slows you down, throw it out the window. If envy cripples your vision, rip it out at the roots. Our transformation in Christ demands nothing less than our full commitment. This process can be very hard. The Christian life is often referred to as a race because we need the discipline and the fortitude of athletes to wage the war against our human frailties. But we will be triumphant.

Our children's leaving home may serve as a vigorous reminder that God is the center of our existence. If we see the change in our lives as a chance to make radical changes in our relationship to Christ, we will not be diminished but rather made splendid.

Perhaps the emptiness does throw us off guard and we are tempted to indulge in self-pity. Perhaps we do feel less attractive, less worthwhile. But, as is true with so much in life, our feelings are not primary. Our actions are. We can frame our lives in such a way that we grow into those things that we should like to be. Remember the movie *The King and I*, starring Yul Brynner and Deborah Kerr? In singing about the fear of the unknown, Deborah Kerr's character offers this

120

counsel: "Make believe you're brave, and the trick will take you far. You may be as brave as you make believe you are." If we *act as if* we are generous, gentle, loving women who embrace the freedoms of the empty nest rather than dread them, we will become that which we pretend to be.

Carlo Caretto explains this concept of *act as if* in his book *In Search of the Beyond*. After encouraging his readers to act bravely even in the midst of difficulties, Caretto writes:

But in order to do this, you will tell me next, one needs faith, and I have so little or none at all. Well, I have a secret I would like to share with you. Only a few will accept what I say, of course, but it is all the same of the utmost importance. The thought comes from Pascal, and I have put it to the test time and time again.

It goes like this: "act as if." I will explain. Are you in trouble, and yet have the feeling that you have not sufficient faith to cope with it? All right then, "act as if" you did have faith and organize the details of your life as if you lived by faith. You will find that everything will work out in accordance with your desire for faith. . . . "Act as if" you possessed utter faith, unbounded hope and endless charity and cast yourself into the fray, not relying on yourself but on the strength that comes to you from your trust in God.

Such a course of action offers endless possibilities. Our feelings will catch up with our actions if we persevere along the path of goodness. We will become that which we seek to be: imitators of Christ Jesus. Christ's actions radiated love. In 1 John 4:16, we read: "We know and rely on the love God has for us. God is love. Whoever lives in love lives in God, and God in him." Even when our feelings are awry, we can act out of our knowledge and belief.

Think about poor, weary Elijah. We read his story in 1 Kings 19. Worn out and dejected, he feels like dying. But God has other plans for him. Elijah has to be reminded to do the most basic things: "Get up and eat, for the journey is too much for you" (v. 7b), God tells him. Elijah retreats to a cave, but God won't let him stay there. Elijah feels like staying in the cave, but through an act of will he obeys the words of the Lord: "Go out and stand on the mountain in the presence of the LORD; for the LORD is about to pass by" (v. 11a). And Elijah is formed by his choices, by those individual steps—"baby steps," if you will—toward God.

I once heard a lay speaker talk about God's searchlight. "Jesus shines a big searchlight into our souls," this woman said. "And he makes us relinquish all those hidden little faults that nobody sees, those little pettinesses that keep us from really imitating him." One by one we turn over those faults to Christ, and we move along the path of spiritual perfection. The transformation does not come to an end. As he did with Elijah, God will always nudge us out of our caves. Always, we can grow in grace and love. Staying open to the working of God in our lives is one of our greatest challenges.

DRAWING CLOSER TO GOD

Many women talked openly with me about their relationship with God. Some acknowledged that their relationship with their creator hasn't changed since their children left home. One woman explained that she has always known that God is power. Now that her children are grown, the patterns of her prayers have not changed. "I just keep making sure to get my kids in those prayers," she told me.

Others recognized a marked alteration. "I pray so much more now," said Cleo. "I'm always praying for my kids. I think God must be asking himself why he gave me so many kids because I'm always bugging him about them." Like Cleo, many women acknowledge that much of their prayer time is spent in petition for their children. "I put their lives in his hands," Gloria told me. "God has to protect them now because I can't."

Another woman knows that her prayer life has deepened her gratitude. "God has made me so thankful," this woman told me. "I had great parents myself. My dad had such a strong faith. When my son got married last year, I sat in the church and realized it had to be one of the best days in my life. God has been so good."

Clarisse, a retired cook, feels the presence of God in her life when her grown children call home and say, "Mom, please pray for this friend of mine. She needs help." Her children know that their mother is a woman of prayer, so they set her to work on the needs of their friends. They say to their classmates. "I'll get my mom to pray for you." Clarisse recalls that on the day her son left home, he held his Bible in his hand and said, "This book is the most important thing I'm taking with me." "My prayer life is very important to me," Clarisse said. "In the morning, I start by talking to God and the conversation sets the tone for the entire day."

In developing our growing relationship with Christ, the "Jesus in my back pocket" mentality sometimes develops. We become so fixated on being good friends with Jesus that we are tempted to make that friendship an end in itself. Like Saint Peter at the Transfigu-

Empty Nest, Full Life

ration, we want to build tents (see Luke 9:28-36).
We're so glad to have Jesus in our back pocket, we forget that our love of Christ is meant to shatter the
hardened and dark places in the universe. Walking
with Jesus alone in the garden while the dew is still
on the roses is fine if it helps us grow in the knowledge of God. That very knowledge, however, demands
that we become the light of the world.

To be sure, in order to become Christlike we have
to walk with him alone. But friendship with Jesus
demands that we become the light of the world. As we
draw closer to God, we feel an increased desire to
reach out to others. And reaching out to others
inevitably pulls us back to God.

If we do not recognize the opportunities in the
empty nest, we will miss one of the greatest chances
life offers us to become Christlike. The spiritual clas-
sic *The Imitation of Christ* by Thomas à Kempis
offers very practical, clearheaded, spiritual direction.
In this book we read:

He who follows Me, says Christ our savior, walks not in
darkness, for he will have the light of life. These are the
words of our Lord Jesus Christ, and by them we are admon-
ished to follow His teachings and His manner of living, if
we would truly be enlightened and delivered from all blindness of heart. Let all study of our heart be from now on to
have our meditation fixed wholly on the life of Christ, for
His Holy teachings are of more virtue and strength than all
the angels and saints . . . we must study to conform our life
as nearly as we can to His.

The only emptiness in such conformation is the
emptying out of self as we make room for the One
who transforms us.

The Nest Is Not Really Empty
IN GOD'S PRESENCE

1) Choose one of the following passages from Mark:
    1:14-22   Call of the Disciples
    1:23-28   Cure of the Demoniac
    2:1-12   Paralytic at Capernaum
    3:1-6   Man with a Withered Hand
    5:1-18   Expulsion of the Devils in Gerasa

2) Read it aloud once. For just a few seconds, try to recreate the scene in your mind.

3) Read the passage aloud again, paying attention to details you might have missed.

4) Then, prayerfully enter into the scene. Listen carefully to the words being spoken. Watch Jesus closely. How does he sound? How is he moving? How does he interact with others? What significance does/can this meditation have for your life? Offer a concluding prayer.

A FINAL WORD

This book began as my attempt to make sense of my own fear and sadness. Writing it has helped me to understand, truly, that there is nothing to fear in the empty nest. There are still moments when my longing for my children overwhelms me. Something as routine as programming my sons' phone numbers into my telephone makes me sad. For eighteen years, I didn't have to phone these fellows. They were in the next room. They no longer are. And I still find it hard to return home with just my husband and daughter after taking the boys back to college after a break.

But the awkwardness passes. Soon, I am not missing their presence as I fall asleep at night. In a little while, I'm no longer listening for the sounds of their turning over in their beds. I have become accustomed to the ebb and flow of having grown children.

I understand that ebb and flow much better now that I've talked to so many other mothers. As I sat in living rooms and at kitchen tables and on sun porches, listening to the stories women told, I came to understand how limited my own understanding of the empty nest had been. So often, I'd walk away from a woman's home and think, "Her life has nothing to do with emptiness."

All of the people who talked to me seemed so shining, so vital, so far from being finished with their lives. They were clear-eyed grandmothers with walls full of family photos to show me. They were mothers who had to have tissue nearby to stave off the tears. They were professionals who talked to me between phone calls. Every single one of them taught me about God. I found myself thinking: How pleased God must be with such people. How much good they still have left to accomplish. How lucky their children are to have such people as mothers.

Never did I walk away from a woman thinking that her task on earth was done. Never did the thought even occur to me that God was finished with these human beings. They were all so busy, actually, that we had difficulty scheduling the interviews. Whether the women were closing in on fifty or eighty, they emanated the love of God. Their nests may have been empty, but their lives were full.

Once again I am reminded of God's glorious message to me at Lake Bassenthwaite in England: *Life is good. And love is endless. And although there is great grief in the world there is much good to be done.* Our lives can prove these words to be true. For, our lives well-lived are their own answers to the empty nest.